PRAISE FOR
I AM
(Transformed in Him)
A Meditative Bible Study – Volume 1

Authors Diana Burg and Kim Tapfer have brought a new perspective on the transformative nature of God in their book I AM. Integrating elements from their own lives and spiritual journeys, they have offered a devotional filled with wisdom, compassion, tenderness and honesty. The reader is led to experience a deeper intimacy in a relationship with God, one where there is a constant reminder that God's word is alive and active in the heart of a believer. I AM reminds us that we can do all things through Christ and that it is never too late to embrace the renewal God offers us daily.
  – Noelle Cablay, Music Artist and Author of Pieces of Sky

Praise the Lord!! It is hard for me to find the words, but I found myself being more open and honest with myself than I have ever been and grew more than I ever expected! This study was so very honest and heartwarming that it allowed me the freedom to be myself and truly express my thoughts without feeling weak or inferior and growing even stronger in the Lord!! Thank you for the openness and honesty and sharing your own courage and growth!!
  – Jayne Hause, One who took the study in spring of 2012

This study will simply nourish and strengthen you! It's one I keep going back to and continue to glean from. Few books bring such clear peace and joy, hope and love. Encased in a multitude of stories and Scripture verses, it speaks volumes of truth! As its meditative questions bid you to move toward personal revelation about who God is to you on a daily basis, the interaction is an amazing, deeply satisfying, one-of-a-kind experience!
  – Nancy Cashen, Bible Study Core Leader, Mariners Church

What a remarkable spiritual odyssey this I AM study recounts! Co-author Diana Burg was once a passionate atheist until God intervened through His Holy Spirit, working through co-author (and Diana's daughter), Kim Tapfer, in bringing Diana to the Lord. Together, mother and daughter have penned a Bible Study that is life-changing and profound. It has my complete endorsement and admiration.
  – Jill Roberts, one who took the study in spring of 2012

I LOVED I AM! It is so sweet and warm and wise! Thank you so much. I learned so much from your choice of Scriptures and from your and Kim's comments. I plan to reread sections of it before I give it to my daughter in law!
  – Lis Pendley, A reader and Burrito Maker for Mean Street Ministry

Being part of helping a mother and daughter, Diana and Kim, put together a Bible study like I AM has strengthened my faith and deepened my relationship with God. I AM is a must read for anyone who wants a closer relationship with God.
  – H. Court Young, Publisher and Author

I AM

(Transformed in Him)
A Meditative Bible Study – Volume 1

I AM

(Transformed in Him)
A Meditative Bible Study – Volume 1

Transforming into the Image of Christ
through the I AM Sayings
in the books of
Exodus, John, and Revelation

VOLUME 1: WEEKS 1-6

by Diana Burg and Kim Tapfer

I AM
(Transformed in Him)
A Meditative Bible Study – Volume 1

©2013, Diana Burg and Kim Tapfer
All Rights Reserved.

Published by:

Healthy Life Press • 2603 Drake Drive • Orlando, FL 32810
www.healthylifepress.com

Cover and Internal Designs: Judy Johnson

Cover photo by West Coast Sea Glass (www.WestCoastSeaGlass.com)

Printed in the United States of America

This book is protected by US copyright laws. It may not be transmitted to others via electronic file or printed copy. Ebook purchasers do have permission to print a copy for your own personal use.

Library of Congress Cataloging-in-Publication Data
Burg, Diana and Kim Tapfer
   I Am – (Transformed in Him) A Meditative Bible Study – Volume 1

ISBN 978-1-939267-52-8
1. Bible Study; 2. Personal Growth; 3. Bible Study-Women

Every attempt has been made to properly identify and credit sources of all quotations cited.

Undesignated Scripture references are taken from THE HOLY BIBLE, NEW INTERNATIONAL VERSION®, NIV®, Copyright© 1973, 1978, 1984, 2011 by Biblica, Inc.™ Scriptures marked NKJV are from the New King James Version, Copyright© 1982 by Thomas Nelson, Inc. Used by permission. All rights reserved worldwide. Capitalization and punctuation follow the source used.

The printed version of this book is available worldwide through bookstores and online outlets and through the publisher, with free shipping. This book is also available from *STL-Distribution.com* as an eBook at: *eChristian.com*, *Amazon.com*, and *BN.com*. It exists in a downloadable and printable PDF format directly from the publisher at: *www.healthylifepress.com*. Visit the authors' website at: *www.transformedinhim.com*. Direct publisher e-mail contact: *dbbv1@aol.com*.

Multiple copy discount available. Contact: *healthylifepress@aol.com* for information. Redistribution of printed or eBook formatted copies violates international copyright law, and is strictly forbidden. Your honesty is appreciated.

DEDICATION

To Charles, my beloved husband, without your love and encouragement I would not be a writer. Our weekend Bible studies have deepened my faith and made me realize that I AM is my all in all, and you are God's gift to me.

– Diana Burg

To my wonderful husband, Ted, whose love and support enabled me to pursue my dream of taking part in I AM. Truly, I could not have done it without you.

– Kim Tapfer

Acknowledgements

Kim Tapfer and Diana Burg want to thank Court and Sharon Young for their invaluable support and critiques, advice, and participation in the publishing process.

We also would like to thank Noelle Cablay, Music Artist and Author of *Pieces of Sky* for her encouragement, advice, and very helpful information throughout the journey of *I AM* to publishing.

We would also like to thank Mary Beth Bueke of West Coast Sea Glass for the beautiful sea glass photograph on the cover and Judy Johnson for her incredible design work on the book and cover.

We also want to express special gratitude to Kim's morning Bible study group for support, prayer, and friendship.

We would like to thank our most gifted and accomplished publisher, Dave Biebel, for the great and generous present to us of his enormous God given talent in publishing. His wisdom, advice and passionate flair for serving the Lord have been an inspiration, an encouragement, and an incomparable support.

Publisher's Notes

1. The cover depicts "sea glass." Sea glass most often comes from broken beer bottles, soda bottles, and other glass objects that the sea has swallowed. When the ocean's powerful waves consistently roll over these shattered shards of glass they are transformed into the most stunningly translucent glass you have ever seen. Much like sea glass, our broken lives can be transformed into something amazingly beautiful in the Lord's hands.

2. The primary voice of this volume is Diana's, though Kim was deeply involved in the writing and the thought behind it. Where Kim is speaking, this is clearly identified.

3. Due to this book's focus on the I AM sayings, most statements that contain this phrase directly relating to deity have been capitalized, even if they are not capitalized in an original source.

Contents

Praise for I AM

Dedication

Acknowledgements

Introduction   2

Week 1   I AM WHO I AM   4

Week 2   Jesus, the Word   34

Week 3   Jesus, the Messiah   78

Week 4   Jesus, the Bread of Life   114

Week 5   Jesus, the Light of the World   150

Week 6   Jesus, the Door to Life   196

About the Authors   238

Notes   240

INTRODUCTION

God first introduces himself to Moses as I AM THAT I AM, or another translation of the name is I AM WHO I AM, the term we will be using in this study. Throughout this six-week study we will begin to unearth the treasure trove of riches that are found within God's name, I AM WHO I AM.

Each week has five days of study. At the end of each day there will be two prompts; 1) **Today's Exercise** and 2) **Prayer**. At the end of every week there will be a **Further Revelation** prompt before the **Weekly Exercise**.

- **Today's Exercise** will be an opportunity for you to journal on that day's reading.
- **Prayer** will be your prayer response to that day's reading.
- **Further Revelation** provides a place to record new insights you have received about our Lord.
- **Weekly Exercise** helps you summarize what you've gained that week.

Within each day there is room for journaling, but you may find that you need more room to record all your thoughts. In this case, you will not only need your Bible but also a notebook. We have used the New International Version from Biblesoft 2006, but use whatever version you want. We want this study to be fulfilling, rewarding, and we want it to have a flow within your daily life. You can do this study anywhere—in the car, in the waiting room, before going to sleep, etc. At the end of every week there is a **Weekly Exercise**.

The point of this study and each weekly exercise is to bring you closer to I AM and to the idea that I AM is everything, our all in all. We have put most of the Bible quotes in the body of this work.

We don't want readers to have to spend a lot of time going between the Bible and this study. We hope this saves a lot of time and gives the study more seamlessness in your life.

The first chapter is devoted to the name God the Father gave to Moses in the Book of Exodus, I AM WHO I AM.

The second chapter is about the absolute usage by Jesus of I AM without the predicate, as in "Before Abraham was I AM" (John 8:58).

The third chapter is about the use of the indirect predicate to refer to Jesus as in the Garden of Gethsemane when Jesus asked the soldiers, "Whom do you seek?" When they answered, "Jesus of Nazareth," Jesus replied, "*I AM He*" (John 18:4-6).

Chapters four through six cover three of the allegorical sayings of Jesus in the Book of John: "I AM the bread of life," "I AM the light of the world," "I AM the door [or the gate]."

More than anything, every day of this study, we want you to come to understand, in the profoundest sense, I AM. We want you to fill out the blank check of who God is to you on a daily basis. Consider both your wants and needs. As you work through this study ask God each day for revelation of who he is to you. Fill out the blank check Hannah Smith talks about in the quote below. As you close each day thank God for what he has revealed to you about his being I AM.

> *I believe it (I AM) includes everything the human heart longs for and needs. This unfinished name of God seems to me like a blank check signed by a rich friend given to us to be filled in with whatever sum we may desire....* [1]

Fill out whatever sum you desire. Use the daily prompts to journal a little about this every day. It can be just a sentence or a novel. It's up to you.

WEEK ONE

I Am Who I Am

*God said to Moses, "I AM WHO I AM.
This is what you are to say to the Israelites:
'I AM has sent me to you.'"* Exodus 3:14

week one

Day 1
THE ETERNAL AND UNCHANGEABLE NATURE OF GOD

Some Sunday mornings my husband, Charles, and I walk in the mountains. We take the Bible and a book called *Christ, The Experience of Jesus as Lord* by Edward Schillebeeckx, a Dutch theologian. It is a time for us of entering the Lord's matrix and walking in his world with him. We feel we both receive great revelation and a sense of walking, strolling really, and talking with him, in the garden of the Colorado foothills. We read a little of Schillebeeckx and then the pertinent Bible passage. I find myself saying quite often, "Oh, I never understood that, but oh that's what it means or

> "God . . . must be the same yesterday, today, and forever, if we are to have any peace or comfort."
> — Hannah Smith

could mean." For example, we were reading about Lazarus, and I said to Charles, "I have always wondered why Jesus wept at the death of Lazarus. I know he has great empathy and compassion, but he knew he would raise Lazarus." Charles thought for a bit as we sat on our bench in Elk Meadow and watched the wildflowers in the sun. Then he answered, with a touch of uncertainty, "I wonder if the Father in Jesus was looking forward to the death of his own Son, a very sorrowful and painful time, which would be his own sacrifice, that he must witness even though he knew he would raise him from the dead." That kind of revelation came to me when we were studying the "I AM" sayings from the book of John, and I felt as Hannah Smith described in *The God of All Comfort*:

> *These simple words, I AM, express therefore eternity and unchangeableness of existence, which is the very first element necessary in a God who is to be depended upon. No dependence could be placed by any one of us upon a changeable God. He must be the same yesterday, today, and forever, if we are to have any peace or comfort.*[1]

God is eternal and unchangeable.

week one

Deuteronomy 33:27: The eternal God is your refuge, and underneath are the everlasting arms.

Psalm 16:11: You have made known to me the path of life; you will fill me with joy in your presence, with eternal pleasures at your right hand.

Isaiah 26:4: Trust in the LORD forever, for the LORD, the LORD, is the Rock eternal.

Daniel 4:3: How great are his signs, how mighty his wonders! His kingdom is an eternal kingdom; his dominion endures from generation to generation.

1 Samuel 15:29: He who is the Glory of Israel does not lie or change his mind; for he is not a man, that he should change his mind.

Malachi 3:6: I the LORD do not change. So you, O descendants of Jacob, are not destroyed.

Hebrews 13:8: Jesus Christ is the same yesterday and today and forever.

Today's Exercise
Review these Scriptures and pick one that is especially meaningful to you today. Why is this passage meaningful to you?

Remember how Hannah Smith beautifully illuminates that the name I AM:

> *. . . includes everything the human heart longs for and needs. This unfinished name of God seems to me like a blank check signed by a rich friend given to us to be filled in with whatever sum we may desire . . . .*[2]

week one

What does your human heart long for and need?

Prayer
Pray for I AM to reveal himself in this way to you today and throughout this study.

Day 2
MOSES MEETS I AM

Quickly review Exodus 1-3 to remind yourself of Moses' early life.

After Moses had left his royal roots, because of murdering an Egyptian abusing one of his fellow Israelites, he became a shepherd. It seemed that Moses was destined to spend the rest of his life tending sheep. In some metaphorical ways that turned out to be his life work, but it was not the four legged variety that he shepherded. His new calling commenced the day when, standing in front of a very ordinary bush, it began to burn and yet not be consumed. And the Lord spoke to him out of the bush. The Lord told Moses that he wanted to deliver his people from the Egyptians, and he said to Moses:

> **Exodus 3:10 (NKJV): "Come now, therefore, and I will send**

week one

you to Pharaoh that you may bring My people, the children of Israel, out of Egypt."

Moses, after briefly protesting, asked "Who are you? What is your name?"

Exodus 3:13-14: "Suppose I go to the Israelites and say to them, 'The God of your fathers has sent me to you,' and they ask me, 'What is his name?' Then what shall I tell them?" God said to Moses, "I AM WHO I AM. This is what you are to say to the Israelites: 'I AM has sent me to you.'"

Although this is the first time Moses was formally introduced to I AM, Exodus 1 and 2 clearly show that I AM was always a part of Moses' life.

"Who are you?" Moses asked God.

Today's Exercise
1. How was God I AM to Moses even before Moses knew him? Think about the period of time from when he was born to the burning bush experience.

2. Do you think of I AM as having always been in your life? How? Give brief descriptions of one or more instances.

Prayer
Praise I AM for how you have seen him working in your life and ask for I AM to continue to show you how he has always been in your life.

Day 3
MORE ON I AM

I AM is more familiar to us as Yahweh and Jehovah. Adam Clarke's Commentary gives an excellent overview of various interpretations of what God meant:

> [I AM THAT I AM] . . . The Vulgate translates . . . <u>"I AM who am."</u> The Septuagint has <u>"I AM He who exists."</u>. . .<u>"The Eternal,"</u> who passes not away; . . . The Targum of Jonathan, and the Jerusalem Targum paraphrase the words thus: <u>"He who spake, and the world was; who spake, and all things existed."</u> As the original words literally signify, <u>"I will be what I will be,"</u> some have supposed that God simply designed to inform Moses, <u>that what he had been to his fathers Abraham, Isaac, and Jacob, he would be to him</u> and the Israelites; and <u>that he would perform the promises he had made to his fathers,</u> by giving

week one

"Whom shall I say has sent me?"

> *their descendants the promised land. It is difficult to put a meaning on the words, they seem intended to point out the eternity and self-existence of God. Plato, in his Parmenides, where he treats sublimely of the nature of God, says, . . . <u>nothing can express his nature; therefore no name can be attributed to him.</u>[3]*

It is true that, before Moses, there was no written word of or about God, and the Israelites had been living amongst the Egyptians for 400 years. Therefore, it is easy to assume that the Israelites' image of God had been blurred. Their image may have morphed into many gods and deities prevalent in the Egyptian culture. All the Egyptian gods had names, and Moses may well himself have thought the burning bush to be a "god" who, for some odd and inexplicable reason, needed a confused, stuttering shepherd to perform his will. Adam Clarke's commentary says:

> *[They shall say to me, What is his name?] Does not this suppose that the Israelites had an idolatrous notion even of the Supreme Being? They had probably drunk deep into the Egyptian superstitions, and had gods many and lords many; and*

I Am Who I Am

> *Moses conjectured that, hearing of a supernatural deliverance, they would inquire who that God was by whom it was to be effected.*[4]

Moses, in asking God's name, may also have been inquiring about his nature, his character. Nelson's *Illustrated Bible Dictionary* teaches us that "the people of the Bible were very conscious of the meaning of names. They believed there was a vital connection between the name and the person it identified. A name somehow represented the nature of the person."[5]

I have always loved Moses' conversations with God. He is, to say the very least, presumptuous. He doesn't mince words. Probably even, he may be a bit sarcastic, "Ok, suppose I do go to the people, just suppose. . . . What am I going to tell them?" It's as if Moses is saying, "Oh boy, this answer better be good, really good, or I'll be in a whole lot of trouble with the Israelites."

Does God chastise Moses? Does he tell him that it's none of his disrespectful business? Not for an eternal second. He says without hesitation, "I AM WHO I AM." Is he speaking just to Moses? Today, in an audience irony, we know very well that our God, our precious Lord, was speaking to all generations, then and now, from Adam and Eve and Abraham to Hannah Smith and the pastor in your church, from the beginning of time to the present day, from forever to forever, to you and me, this very minute.

week one

Importantly, God tells Moses that this name is God's name "forever," and that God is to be remembered by this from "generation to generation" (Exodus 3:15). This name of God was given to Moses and the Israelites as a name of deliverance, but is also a name of deliverance for all God's people for all generations. It is a name of deliverance for us!

> **Today's Exercise**
> Think about I AM as Yahweh and the underlined definitions described in Adam Clarke's commentary. Meditate on the eternity and self-existence of God. What does this mean for our lives?
>
> 1. God says only that he is I AM. He does not amplify. He could have said, "I AM loving; I AM good; I AM all powerful." But he doesn't. Why do you think he does not? What does this mean for us?

I Am Who I Am

2. Look up Genesis 28:13,15; Psalm 81:10; Isaiah 45:5, 6, 18, 22; Isaiah 47:8, 10. How does God finish the I AM statements? Record below.

What is the most meaningful of these descriptions of God to you today? And why?

Prayer
Pray for I AM to reveal himself in this way to you today and throughout this study.

Day 4
Universal Meanings and Attributes of I AM

How do the universal implications, the meanings, the attributes which characterize God's name, I AM, affect Moses, the Israelites, and . . . us? Let's take a look at a few of the inferences about his name, I AM.

1. **God's relationship to humanity is personal and intimate.** When I was growing up my father would often read the Bible to me but expressed his feeling that God no longer interacted with man. He thought of God as a kind of heavenly whirlwind, swirling about the heavens, uninterested and deliberately detached from man on earth. Dad thought God's relationship to humans commenced after our death. Because of my father's influence, at first,

in my youth, God became irrelevant. Then, in college, he became non-existent, an imaginary tool for those too weak to face the existential truth and reality of existence. I agreed with Karl Marx that religion was the opium of the masses. We were here alone and would suffer the egregious indignity of eternal and meaningless life and death.

"What's in a name?" Juliet asked Romeo. Frankly, who cares if you are never going to get to know the person or even make the acquaintance? But if God is the God of history, actively involved in the destiny of humanity, as well as intimately in control of every life, then each moment of existence becomes pivotal and significant, dependent upon who God is. The name, I AM, connotes such a relationship with people, with the Israelites, with Moses. God is saying to Moses, not only that he was the God of their forefathers, but that he was "I AM" when Moses was formed in the womb, floated in the bulrushes, raised by Pharaoh's daughter and standing before him at the burning bush. I AM was always involved in his life, in the lives of his forebears and would forever be a part of, in fact, *in control of* their future destiny, fortunes and circumstances. And God does not shout from afar. He doesn't wave his hands for attention from some distant shore, or stand in a fiery chariot watching but not speaking. He deals with Moses, face to face, mano a mano, friend to friend. Is there any greater intimacy possible?

2. **God is the present tense forever.** When I was working with an editor on an early book of mine about getting to know God, I frequently used the term "God was." I would say something like, "Mary Jane was sick but believed God was healing her." The editor called me and said, "I'm not comfortable with your saying, 'God was.' I want you to change that to 'God is,' or some form of the present tense."

My first thought was, "He must be kidding. You can't say, 'Mary Jane was sick but believed God is healing her.'" I wanted to ask, "Are you crazy?" But he insisted vehemently, "God never 'was' in the past imperfect or past perfect tense. He always *is*, and you will have to find a way to deal with it." I probably, in my new Christianity, would have been sarcastic if I weren't so shocked. I was not only baffled but a little scared that there would be no way to the present tense forever. But then 'I AM' showed me a path through the 'HE WAS' forest.

> **Mary Jane was very sick but she was a great believer in God's healing and told me, "God is healing me all the time."**

So I learned the hard way that the present tense signifies the eternal and unalterable nature of God. This can be expressed in a kind of build-a-bear sentence or a dance in rondo. God always was. God always was and is. God always was, is, and will be. God always was, is, and will be the same forever.

3. **I AM denotes total self-sufficiency.** The simple declarative clause 'I AM,' excludes as many possibilities as it engenders about the nature of God. It excludes the possibility of dependence upon anyone else, heavenly or earthly, for his existence or his nature. It excludes any action of his or any part of his character based upon someone else's grace or creativity. In fact, it excludes the idea of any comparable being, always remembering the triune God is one person.

So his total self-dependence and self-sufficiency mean that his nature is absolute—absolute responsibility and independence in all his actions, whether the creation of the world and humanity or the interaction of world events or even the formation of you and me.

4. **God is the "omni" of everything, earthly and heavenly.** "Omni" in combination with other words is derived from the Latin root meaning "all." With his name, I AM, God then embodies every godly attribute as self-contained, complete, incarnate truth. He is all powerful, omnipotent and all knowing, omniscient. He is the "all in all." It means that he is the Alpha and Omega (the beginning and the end of the Greek alphabet) of everything, from creation to the end of the world.

5. **God has sovereign liberty to act on behalf of humankind.**

> Exodus 33:19: ". . . I give grace to whom I please, and I show mercy to whom I please."

I Am Who I Am

Nothing compels I AM to act on behalf of man or in judgment against him. The idea of the complete freedom of God in bestowal of grace and mercy, also favor, is a complex and paradoxical concept. When God gives his grace and mercy to the Israelites under Moses, to what has he elevated humanity? When we live under grace and mercy, God has shortened the distance and cured the huge imbalance and disequilibrium between humanity and God.

> Exodus 33:12-14: Moses said to the LORD, "You have been telling me, 'Lead these people,' but you have not let me know whom you will send with me. You have said, 'I know you by name and you have found favor with me.' If you are pleased with me, teach me your ways so I may know you and continue to find favor with you. Remember that this nation is your people." The LORD replied, "My Presence will go with you, and I will give you rest."

Edward Schillebeeckx says that this text is characteristic of the idea of grace in the Old Testament. What we receive from God, what closes the distance between God and humanity is:

week one

> *. . . election, favour, setting out together, mutual knowledge of each other's name, the use of familiar forms of address, God's countenance which is turned towards men, towards Israel. . . .*[6]

So, with Moses and with us, what God has chosen I AM to mean is free and unconstrained grace, which is unmerited sanctification of humankind.

6. **I AM is a covenant God who keeps his promises always.** When God first introduces himself to Moses, he says:

> **Exodus 3:6: I AM the God of thy father, the God of Abraham, the God of Isaac, and the God of Jacob.**

I AM the God of thy father. God here explains, in an historical, evidentiary way, his covenant with Moses and his people. He is the father of Moses' father, Amram, as well as the patriarchs, with whom he had a covenant, kept the covenant, and now would continue to keep the covenant in a direct historical descent. He was announcing himself to Moses as a God who keeps his promises. If I think of myself as Moses, and what it would take to convince me, not just of God's good will and ability to keep his promises, but my authority and ability to act on his behalf, I would have to be certain:

I Am Who I Am

    a. that God had kept his promises.
    b. that he would teach me and guide me as to my part in performing on his behalf.
    c. that he would go with me as an all powerful God.
    d. that I would be the same kind of heir to the promises as Abraham, Isaac, and Jacob.

I AM gives all the assurances by describing himself as the God of Moses' father and all the patriarchs on the family tree.

> **Today's Exercise**
> Today we read about six universal meanings and attributes of I AM.
>
> 1. I AM's relationship to humanity is personal and intimate.
> 2. I AM is the present tense forever.
> 3. I AM denotes total self-sufficiency.
> 4. I AM is the "omni" of everything, earthly *and* heavenly.
> 5. I AM has sovereign liberty to act on behalf of man.
> 6. I AM is a covenant God who keeps his promises always.

week one

What is the most meaningful attribute to you today and why?

Prayer
Pray for I AM to reveal himself in this way to you today and throughout this study.

Day 5
JESUS AS I AM

Every fulfillment of the Old Testament I AM is found in the New Testament Jesus the Christ. In the Book of John, from the first words, we understand the pre-existence and Godhood of Jesus.

> John 1:1-4: In the beginning was the Word, and the Word was with God, and the Word was God. He was with God in the beginning. Through him all things were made; without him nothing was made that has been made. In him was life, and that life was the light of men.

What distinguishes Christianity from other religions is that we believe Jesus is God and that he came down from heaven to be, among other job descriptions, our salvation and mediation between heaven and earth. In the Old Testament Book of Exodus, I AM came to Moses to primarily effect the liberation of his people, the Israelites. Jesus came for us all, everyone, and he does not want anyone to remain lost.

week one

2 Peter 3:9: The Lord is not slow in keeping his promise, as some understand slowness. He is patient with you, not wanting anyone to perish, but everyone to come to repentance.

The new covenant who is our Lord Jesus Christ, is salvation and eternal life for ALL who choose him.

I am an alcoholic and drug addict, sober and clean now for over thirty years, but I have not forgotten my past. If I had to pick one description of my past life to define what I was trying to heal with the drugs and alcohol, it would be "alienation." I used drugs and alcohol, paradoxically, to find reconciliation with my world, friends, family, life, environs, and myself. Enormous fear accompanied that sense of alienation, loneliness, and separateness from all things. I was an atheist, but powerless within myself to overcome that agonizing, all encompassing estrangement.

Of course, drugs and alcohol make the user worse and far more alienated. No one could stand my drinking. My husband left me; a neighbor confronted me; my daughter wept as she declared me lost; a friend was lifting me up in her prayer group; and, my assistant at work quit because of my drinking. Yet, I gave a devotion to the alcohol like Jezebel gave to Baal–uninterrupted passion, allegiance, adoration, and worship, defending to the death

I had to find another God . . . the Lord Jesus, the new covenant God, who died for me on a cross, who replaced all my alienation with reconciliation.

against all comers. But alcohol didn't even keep its promises. Toward the end of my drinking I couldn't get drunk or high on pills; I began to hallucinate and lose motor function. I couldn't even commit suicide, at least, in any kind of instant way.

I had to find another God. You guessed it! Through AA and my daughter I found the Lord Jesus, the new covenant God, who died for me on a cross, who replaced all my alienation with reconciliation. He taught me that I AM would answer my longing and question, "What am I thirsty for?" with I AM as the Living Water that flows eternally. Jesus becomes for all believers better than the replacement for our false idols; he becomes our everything, as Hannah Smith describes in The God of All Comfort:

> *Every attribute of God, every revelation of His character, every proof of His undying love, every declaration of His watchful care, every assertion of His purposes of tender mercy, every manifestation of His loving kindness-all are the filling out of this unfinished "I AM."*[7]

week one

Today's Exercise
In what ways do you need Jesus' loving kindness, tender mercy, watchful care today?

Prayer
Pray for Jesus to reveal himself in this way to you today and throughout this study.

Further Revelation
Write down any answers you had to prayer this week. What new revelations did you receive about our Lord? Write down any thoughts you have about this week.

Weekly Exercise
Briefly review your journal answers at the end of each day and then take a walk with I AM. Think of this walk as a time to just enjoy I AM. Talk with I AM. Talk about anything you want—the beauty of creation, about who he is, about who you are, and about your relationship with him. Lis-

week one

ten and look for I AM along your walk. Be sure that you don't talk the whole time, but be intentional about listening to his voice during your walk.

Journal about your walk here.

WEEK TWO

Jesus, the Word

*In the beginning was the Word,
and the Word was with God,
and the Word was God. John 1:1*

week two

Day 1
JESUS, THE WORD

Just as I was beginning to believe in God, through my sponsor in AA, I began to notice something very odd going on in my house. My daughter had become a Christian. Her reading of the Bible and church going with a friend ought to have been a dead giveaway. Welcome to my world of alcoholic denial! Besides, she never proselytized. But one day, as she saw my belief growing, she asked me, almost casually, to look into the possibility that Jesus was God and Lord and Savior and offered eternal life. I could barely face getting through the day, but I promised I would look into it at some point, perhaps *way* in the future.

OK, I decided, *what could it hurt to check out the possibilities sooner rather than later? I did give my word, and just maybe there might be some advantage to knowing Jesus as Lord and Savior.* So one day I went to a little chapel near our house. I sat in a pew, and I said out loud, "Jesus, if you are Lord and Savior, you are going to have to show me because otherwise I'll never believe." As the word "believe" was hanging on my lips like a cracker crumb, at that very moment, something like a cloud fell on me, and I was encased in the greatest peace, love, and joy I had ever felt. I wanted to spend my life there, get some really plush cushions for the pew, a little camper stove for the altar, a down filled mattress by the stained glass window. I wanted to feel like this forever. I had met I AM, and I knew beyond a shadow of a doubt that my question, my honest prayer, had been answered for eternity. I had learned, in an instant, the truth of the Godhood of Jesus Christ. I wanted everyone to know and build on my experience. Unfortunately, I rather suspect that most people are not going to take my word for it even though my utter sincerity attests.

In my opinion, as well as from my firsthand knowledge, the only way to I AM is to taste, encounter, meet, and finally savor I AM for oneself just as Moses did in the Old Testament. I think of Hitchcock's movie, *The Birds*. All the ads, at the time, advertised with arresting appeal because of the incorrect grammar, "The Birds is coming." In the same way each individual must fill out the predicate to I AM. We must be able to say, "To me, I AM is. I AM is comfort, joy, peace," etc. The presence as well as the present tense "foreverness" of God must be experienced by each individual giving one's life to him. For his or her own self each person must:

> **Psalm 34:8: Taste and see that the LORD is good; blessed is**

> the man who takes refuge in
> him.

How do we come, each one for ourselves, to taste and see that the Lord is good? For me it is a condition for taking refuge in him and understanding his I AM-NESS. There is only one way if the Bible is to be believed.

> **John 14:6: Jesus answered, "I AM the way and the truth and the life. No one comes to the Father except through me."**

If the unequivocal nature of this statement is true then the first questions are, "Who is Jesus? Who does Jesus say he is? Does he identify himself as I AM and in what context?"

The Gospel of John, from its first penned Words, answers unequivocally these questions.

> **John 1:1-3: In the beginning was the Word, and the Word was with God, and the Word was God. He was with God in the beginning. Through him all things were made; without him nothing was made that has been made.**

Though Jesus is not mentioned by name in this passage, he is identified as God, self existent, responsible for creation, and part of the triune Godhead.

Jesus, the Word

> How do we come, each one for ourselves, to taste and see that the Lord is good? For me it is a condition for taking refuge in him and understanding his I AM-NESS.

1. **Jesus is the beginning.** The first words of the Gospel of John start with, "In the Beginning." Jesus tells us, in the final chapter of Revelation, that "I AM the Alpha and the Omega, the First and the Last, the Beginning and the End" (Revelation 22:12-13). There has never been a "before Jesus;" he has always been. At certain times in our lives we can struggle with a beginning. We may question, say, "When will he propose?" "When will I get a job?" "When will I have a baby?" "When will I be healed?" Grasping hold of the truth that Jesus is "the beginning" pierces us with the truth that he is more than equipped to determine all of our beginnings.

2. **Jesus is "THE."** For instance, Jesus is THE Word. There is only one Word, Jesus is the only Word, singular and preeminent in nature. In a later chapter we have an extended discussion on the word "THE" in the I AM sayings.

But for now, what does it mean that Jesus is "the Word"?

The Word was a term used by theologians and philosophers, both Jews and Greeks, in many different ways. In Hebrew Scripture the Word was an agent of creation (Psalm 33:6), the source of God's message to his people through the prophets (Hosea 1:2), and God's law, his standard of holiness (Psalm 199:11). In Greek philosophy,

> *the Word was the principle of reason that governed the world, or the thought still in the mind, while in Hebrew thought, the Word was another expression for God . . .*[1]

3. **Jesus is "WITH" God.** The reader is told two times within the first two verses of John's gospel that the Word was with God. On the one hand this "with" reveals that Jesus was separate and distinct from God, but on the other hand this "with" also points to the relationship between God and the Word. The Greek preposition "with" used in these verses actually means "in communion," thus illuminating the fellowship between God and the Word. John's use of the word "with" within the first two sentences is a sneak peek, a foretaste of this gospel's profound revelation of the deep companionship between Jesus the Son, God the Father, and the Holy Spirit and their unfathomable desire to have us share in their communion.

4. **Jesus is God.** John 1:1 asserts that Jesus had authority commensurate with God the Father. He was with God the Father, and he was God as a separate and distinct entity. The Word is God, again pointing to the mystery of the Trinity. There is only one God, yet three separate and distinct persons within the Godhead—God the Father, God the Son, and God the Holy Spirit. The NIV Life Application Bible Commentary says: "The Hebrew word

for God in Genesis 1:1 is Elohim, a word that speaks of three or more. The use of Elohim then, as far back as Genesis, hints at the mystery of the Trinity. Its use by John reiterates the reality of the Trinity."[2]

5. **Jesus is Creator.** John 1:2 leaves no doubt that Jesus is creator of all things.

Today's Exercise
John 1:1-2 reveals the "withness" of Jesus. The Word was with God the Father, meaning the Word was in communion with God the Father. Amazingly, not only are Jesus and God the Father with each other, but we, as Christ's followers, are invited into this same communion. God desires to be with you for eternity.

Review the following Scriptures and circle one that is especially meaningful to you today.

> John 14:3: "And if I go and prepare a place for you, I will come back and take you to be with me that you also may be where I am."

> John 14:16-17: "And I will ask the Father, and he will give you another Counselor to be with you forever—the Spirit of truth. The world cannot accept him, because it neither sees him nor knows him. But you know him, for he lives with you and will be in you."

> John 14:23: Jesus replied, "If anyone loves me, he will

JESUS, THE WORD

obey my teaching. My Father will love him, and we will come to him and make our home with him."

John 17:24: "Father, I want those you have given me to be with me where I am, and to see my glory, the glory you have given me because you loved me before the creation of the world."

Revelation 3:20-21: "Here I am! I stand at the door and knock. If anyone hears my voice and opens the door, I will come in and eat with him, and he with me. To him who overcomes, I will give the right to sit with me on my throne, just as I overcame and sat down with my Father on his throne."

Why is this passage especially meaningful to you?

week two

Think about the day you have ahead of you. How do you need Jesus to be **with** you?

Prayer
Write a prayer to Jesus asking him to be **with** you in the ways you described in Today's Exercise.

Day 2
No Place Like Home

The Word became flesh and made his dwelling among us. We have seen his glory, the glory of the One and Only, who came from the Father, full of grace and truth.
John 1:14

As a writer, words are very important to me. Well, in fact, they are the whole ball game. I AM, for me, is all the words of God's existence, and yes, all human existence. I AM is the word, is all the words of God here, now, and forever. He is not only telling the story of his life but my life, and the story of his love through all the lives of Christians. The Word became flesh, dwelt among us, died for us, and lives within us if we choose.

The book of Hebrews explains why it was so important that Jesus became flesh, became fully human.

week two

> Hebrews 2:14, 18: Since the children have flesh and blood, he too shared in their humanity so that by his death he might destroy him who holds the power of death—that is, the devil. . . . Because he himself suffered when he was tempted, he is able to help those who are being tempted.

Not only was Jesus fully human, he was also fully God. Jesus existed before all creation; he is, in fact, the beginning, thus establishing his eternal nature. His eternal power is established in that all things were created through him and by him. John chapter one sets the stage for Jesus' own avowal of his Godhood, that he is I AM. There are several ways in which Jesus avers that he is I AM. First, he states he is I AM without the use of any predicate. He says it in the same exact manner as when God spoke to Moses from the burning bush.

> John 8:23-24 (NKJV): And He said to them, "You are from beneath; I AM from above. You are of this world; I AM not of this world. Therefore I said to you that you will die in your sins; for if you do not believe that I AM (He), you will die in your sins."

1. **"From above" means that Jesus is from another physical place, entirely different from this earth, this world.** Clearly, being from this physical world is a more lowly origin. We know that Jesus was both fully human and divine. But he emanates, in fact, emigrates, relocates from another country, heaven, to become human. It is with Jesus, as with the émigrés from any country whose main identification is with their country of origin as well as ancestry. Jesus is from another place that would always be his home. When he says, "I am not of this world," he means that his residence eternally is actually Heaven, a higher place both physically and spiritually.

2. **Jesus contrasts his divine nature with fallen human nature.** What is our human nature? Without God, we feel free to pursue, unfettered, all our bodily desires. Among mine were wealth, alcohol and drugs, and praise from people, to mention only a few of my false idols. My spiritual home, upon which all my affections were focused, was like a Roman palace built for pleasure. In one way or another, without God, all our spiritual homes are built on selfishness and greed and a stinginess with what belongs to us.

Jesus, as human, as flesh, on the other hand, is entirely consumed with Heavenly pursuits. He is utterly dead to the sins of human nature like greed and praise from man. He is telling us that our spiritual temperaments are not just different, but the opposite of his. He is saying that our basic nature is sinful. Spiritually, his nature is heavenly, without sin.

3. **Jesus is the Messiah. He is the I AM who came to save us.**

> John 8:24: ". . . for if you do not believe that I AM (He), you will die in your sins."

So, go ahead, Diana, just stay in your selfishness and greed, in that beautiful little palace, with all its Corinthian pillars and marble staircases, just adjacent to the Roman Forum. You will die there! You will never find your eternal residence! This means, that without Jesus, without the Messiah, without I AM, I can never emigrate to a heavenly home.

4. **We will die in our sins if we do not believe that Jesus is I AM.** Before I became a Christian, as I watched Christians, friends and acquaintances, I thought many unkind things, and developed many aversions to Christians. They were judgmental, arrogant, narrow minded, legalistic, and jingoistic. I got sick of, "Hate the sin, love the sinner." I could readily sympathize, even empathize, with the slogan and bumper sticker mentality, "I'm a born again Pagan." Christians lumped all non-believers together and seemed unable to make distinctions between them. But, of course, the amazing, phenomenal truth is that once we believe that Jesus is I AM we are no longer dead in our sins. That's it! Naturally, it follows as a jet stream from a jet, that real belief in Jesus will bring changes, transformations, ex-

week two

> The amazing, phenomenal truth is that once we believe that Jesus is I AM we are no longer dead in our sins.

planations, and nuances of revelations for a believer. But, like the thief on the cross, if you know, are cognizant of, and convinced of nothing else but that Jesus is I AM, and you give your life to him, you will be with him in heaven.

Jesus left his home from above to come to this fallen world to rescue us so that we could be with him forever in our heavenly home. The word "home" calls to us to our deepest desires, our longing for a place of love, belonging, comfort, rest, laughter, pleasure. Throughout Scripture God beckons us to meditate on our heavenly home, to be mindful that we are merely pilgrims passing through this fallen place.

> **Revelation 21:4: He will wipe every tear from their eyes. There will be no more death or mourning or crying or pain, for the old order of things has passed away.**
>
> **Jeremiah 31:12: They will come and shout for joy on the heights of Zion; they will rejoice in the bounty of the LORD—the grain, the new wine and the oil, the young of the flocks and herds. They will be like a well- watered garden, and they will sorrow no more.**

week two

Isaiah 25:7-8: On this mountain he will destroy the shroud that enfolds all peoples, the sheet that covers all nations; he will swallow up death forever. The Sovereign LORD will wipe away the tears from all faces; he will remove the disgrace of his people from all the earth. The LORD has spoken.

Zephaniah 3:20: At that time I will gather you; at that time I will bring you home. I will give you honor and praise among all the peoples of the earth when I restore your fortunes before your very eyes, says the LORD.

John 14:1-4: Do not let your hearts be troubled. Trust in God; trust also in me. In my Father's house are many rooms; if it were not so, I would have told you. I am going there to prepare a place for you. And if I go and prepare a place for you, I will come back and take you to be with me that you also may be where I am. You know the way to the place where I am going.

Today's Exercise
Review these Scriptures and circle one that is especially meaningful to you today. Why is this passage meaningful to you?

What about your heavenly home are you longing for?

Be especially mindful today of your heavenly home. Think of it often—maybe even put a sticky note on your computer or in some other conspicuous place to constantly remind you about your true home in heaven.

Prayer
Write a prayer to Jesus, thanking him that this is not our home and that he is even, right this moment, preparing a place just for you in heaven.

Day 3
JESUS IS GOD,

Attested to by His Death and Resurrection and He is One with God the Father

In the eighth chapter of John, Jesus again calls himself I AM.

> John 8:28: So Jesus said, "When you have lifted up the Son of Man, then you will know that I AM [the one I claim to be] and that I do nothing on my own but speak just what the Father has taught me."

> John 8:28, KJV: Then said Jesus unto them, "When ye have lifted up the Son of man, then shall ye know that I AM (he), and that I do nothing of myself; but as my Father hath taught me, I speak these things."

I include here both the New International Version and the King James Version because both versions parenthetically include the idea that Jesus is the one he claims to be, and he claims to be God and the Messiah.

1. **Jesus' death and resurrection will convince men of his Godhood.** In the Old Testament when a sacrifice was made it was said to be lifted up or elevated, very much alive before its death. Christ is our perfect sacrificial lamb. Matthew Henry, in his commentary, says:

> *When you have lifted up the Son of man, lifted him up upon the cross, as the brazen serpent upon the pole (John 3:14), as the sacrifices under the law (for Christ is the great sacrifice), which, when they were offered, were said to be elevated, or lifted up; hence the burnt-offerings, the most ancient and honourable of all, were called elevations . . . and in many other offerings they used the significant ceremony of heaving the sacrifice up, and moving it before the Lord; thus was Christ lifted up. Or the expression denotes that his death was his exaltation. They that put him to death thought thereby for ever to have sunk him and his interest, but it proved to be the advancement of both.*[3]

JESUS, THE WORD

> The sacrificial death of Jesus would have been virtually insignificant and purposeless without the resurrection.

In thinking about our, humanity's lifting up of the Son of man, I believe that the lifting of the cross would be utterly meaningless apart from the resurrection. Jesus must be resurrected to complete the meaning of his life and divinity. When Jesus said in John 8:28, "When you have lifted up the Son of Man . . ." he intended the lifting of the cross and his death to signify the spiritual completion of his life, his resurrection. The sacrificial death of Jesus would have been virtually insignificant and purposeless without the resurrection. The weight of all evidence, beyond any reasonable doubt, that Jesus' death atoned for the sins of the world, was his actual resurrection, the deed completed, his scandalous (God becoming man) humanity vindicated, Jesus ". . . seated at the right hand of the heavenly realms, far above all rule and authority, power and dominion, and every title that can be given . . ." (Ephesians 1:20-21).

2. **Jesus did nothing on his own in his human life.** He always did and spoke what the Father taught him. He had total humility. Imagine God coming to earth with all the desires, temptations, lures to which all humans are subjected! Think of what it would be like to subordinate all pull and attraction of the flesh to our Heavenly Father! I cannot get through a day without acting on some aspect of self-will, selfishness, or misguided notion of what's good and right for another person, even though, thanks to the Lord Jesus, I have the precious heavenly kingdom within. I AM

to I AM, human Jesus to God, the Lord Jesus relied always on God the Father to be with him throughout his earthly undertaking and enterprise of reconciling man to God. Jesus always depended completely on God the Father as the instigator, generator, author, and cause of every word and deed. He depended on God the Father's faithfulness, moment by moment, to conduct his mission as Messiah, here on earth. The Father's encouragement, divine grace, and favor always cleared the way, authorized, testified, and glorified the work of Jesus, which glorified the Father. Never for a moment did the Father fail the Son, and vice versa. Matthew Henry, in his commentary states:

> *The King of kings accompanied his own ambassador, to attest his mission and assist his management, and never left him alone, either solitary or weak;*[4]

So Christ is. HE IS Lord and Savior, who always works in conjunction with and in subordination to the Father. What is so striking about God the Son is that now we have, not just paragons like Moses, Joseph, David to emulate, we have God himself to show us precisely the way to heavenly union and existence here on earth. In this troubled and evil world, we gain, not just spiritual insight into how we should exist and survive, but the truth of the one and only God, I AM, living within us. So

Jesus, the Word

Jesus IS, not just a description of I AM as we receive from the Old Testament patriarchs and prophets, he is the fulfillment, completion, and living truth of WHO GOD IS.

Think of it! Jesus, fully God, humbled himself to be taught by the Father. Like Jesus, each day we need to be open to the Father's teaching. As we close today, meditate on this beautiful Psalm.

> **Psalm 119:102-105:** I have not departed from your laws, for you yourself have taught me. How sweet are your words to my taste, sweeter than honey to my mouth! I gain understanding from your precepts; therefore I hate every wrong path.

week two

Today's Exercise
What Scripture has been especially meaningful to you this last week? It may be helpful to review your answers to each day's homework. Write this Scripture below. (It does not have to be verbatim.)

Prayer
Pray and ask God to show you what he is trying to teach you with this Scripture. Write your impressions below and meditate on this Scripture throughout this day.

Day 4
JESUS IS THE OLD TESTAMENT I AM

In John 8:58, we have Jesus' most unequivocal statement of his Godhood.

> "I tell you the truth," Jesus answered, "before Abraham was born, I AM!"

1. **In what context did Jesus make this statement?** As he talked with the Jews, elders, teachers, priests, and moral leaders of the synagogues in his day, he declared himself to be God, Yahweh, Jehovah, with a very clear historical reference to Abraham, whom they considered to be the father of their faith. Jesus had just told them that Abraham rejoiced at the thought of seeing Jesus' day, that he did see it and was glad.

John 8:56 "Your father Abraham rejoiced at the thought of seeing my day; he saw it and was glad."

The Jews had no doubt that Jesus was talking about himself as Messiah and as I AM, God. Jesus may have been speaking about Abraham's joy in the past at the prospect of a Messiah, which Jesus now fulfills. He may have been denoting that he was the incarnation of the God, Yahweh, I AM, who made the promises to Abraham in Genesis 3, 12, and 18. He may, in fact, have been saying that he, Jesus, made the promises. Also, Abraham personally lived out the salvation story when God asked Abraham to sacrifice his only son, Isaac, in Genesis 22. (Briefly review Genesis 22 if this passage of Scripture is unfamiliar to you.)

Certainly Abraham, probably more than any other person within all of Scripture, understood the incredible sacrifice our Heavenly Father would make when he sacrificed his only Son, Jesus, to atone for our sins. But Abraham did not, of course, know this at the time. He made the journey in obedience, trust and allegiance to God, elements of friendship essential in discipleship, and always, of course, attributes forever present in our Lord Jesus. In Genesis 22, Abraham, like God our Father, placed wood on the back of his only son, the son whom he loved. He did this in obedience to the Lord and walked his son, Isaac, up a mountain in Moriah. It is thought that Isaac

JESUS, THE WORD

There can be no doubt that Jesus' claim was that he was God and not just any God but I AM.

was in his early thirties when he made this journey with his father. So he must have known and agreed to this journey with his father, although he did not understand that he was to be the sacrifice.

> **Genesis 22:6-8:** Abraham took the wood for the burnt offering and placed it on his son Isaac, and he himself carried the fire and the knife. As the two of them went on together, Isaac spoke up and said to his father Abraham, "Father?" "Yes, my son?" Abraham replied. "The fire and wood are here," Isaac said, "but where is the lamb for the burnt offering?" Abraham answered, "God himself will provide the lamb for the burnt offering, my son." And the two of them went on together.

God provided for Abraham a ram, an innocent, substitutionary offering for the death of Isaac. The ram was trapped by its horns in a thicket full of thorns (thorns representing the curse of sin) so that Isaac would not have to die; instead, the ram would die in his place. On this third day of the journey, Abraham, figuratively speaking, received Isaac back from the dead because of the sacrifice of the ram (Hebrews 11:17-19). This is an almost exact physical duplication of God the Father's sac-

week two

rifice of Jesus on the cross, except, of course, that Jesus' death on the cross was actual and that he knew he must die and knew his death would be an atonement for the sins of all humanity and that there would be no substitution of an animal for him. God furnished Jesus, the lamb and ram of God (John 1:29), who was without sin (2 Corinthians 5:21), the horn of our salvation (Luke 1:69), cursed by our sin, whose head was crowned with thorns, who died on a cross in our place. And so, too, on the third day God received us back from the dead because of Jesus' death on the cross and resurrection (see 2 Corinthians 5:20-21). The incredible, unmistakable plan of salvation was revealed to Abraham. And Abraham "rejoiced at the thought of seeing my (Jesus') day; he saw it and was glad" (John 8:56).

Adam Clarke, in commenting on this portion of Scripture, states:

> *[Abraham rejoiced to see my day] Or, he earnestly desired to see my day; . . .), I leap—his soul leaped forward in earnest hope and strong expectation that he might see the incarnation of Jesus Christ. The metaphor appears to be taken from a person who, desiring to see a long-expected friend who is coming, runs forward, now and then jumping up to see if he can discover him . . .*[5]

2. We know that the Jews understood the claims, contentions, and reasoning of Jesus because they sought to stone him for his blasphemy that before Abraham was, JESUS IS. Jesus was not just averring some claim to spiritual pre-existence as a blithe, perhaps angelic wraith which, while maybe fantastic, would still not be blasphemous. But the Jews fully understood this was not the claim of Jesus. Jesus was saying, without an ounce of evasion or equivocation, that he was God.

> John 8:59: At this, they picked up stones to stone him, but Jesus hid himself, slipping away from the temple grounds.

There can be no doubt that Jesus' claim was that he was God and not just any God but I AM.

We can learn so much from Abraham for he rejoiced in our salvation. "Rejoice" is a powerful word; it means exceeding joy—not just joy but jumping for joy. When we face problems in life, even those that overwhelm us, we can discover, like Abraham did, that we can always, regardless of our state, rejoice in our salvation. Review the following Scriptures calling us to rejoice.

> Habakkuk 3:18-19: yet I will rejoice in the LORD, I will be joyful in God my Savior. The Sovereign LORD is my strength; he makes my feet

like the feet of a deer, he enables me to go on the heights.

Luke 6:22-23: "Blessed are you when men hate you, when they exclude you and insult you and reject your name as evil, because of the Son of Man. Rejoice in that day and leap for joy, because great is your reward in heaven."

Romans 5:2-4: . . . through whom we have gained access by faith into this grace in which we now stand. And we rejoice in the hope of the glory of God. Not only so, but we also rejoice in our sufferings, because we know that suffering produces perseverance; perseverance, character; and character, hope.

Philippians 4:4: Rejoice in the Lord always. I will say it again: Rejoice!

1 Peter 1:6-7: In this you greatly rejoice, though now for a little while you may have had to suffer grief in all kinds of trials. These have come so that your faith—of greater

worth than gold, which perishes even though refined by fire—may be proved genuine and may result in praise, glory and honor when Jesus Christ is revealed.

week two

Today's Exercise
Circle the Scripture above that is especially meaningful to you today. Why is this Scripture meaningful to you today?

Prayer
Pray and ask God to give you a rejoicing heart because of your salvation.

Day 5
JESUS AS PROPHET

A role of Jesus not often discussed is that of "prophet." Yet, I believe it was one of the most important functions of his ministry here on earth. One can say until the cows come home that I AM God. New Age philosophy often espouses this. But saying it does not make it so. The cross of Christ would, indeed, be as meaningless as the cross of the mocking thief, if Christ's predictions and prophetic message about his mission and his place in spiritual history had not come true. The whole meaning of Christianity rests on the truth of Christ's being who he said he was and accomplishing what he prophesied.

The last I AM saying to be discussed in this week's studies comprehends and affirms all Jesus' previous references to himself as God. This I AM saying occurs after the famous foot washing in the Upper Room.

> John 13:12-17: When he had finished washing their feet, he put on his clothes and returned

> to his place. "Do you understand what I have done for you?" he asked them. "You call me 'Teacher' and 'Lord,' and rightly so, for that is what I AM. Now that I, your Lord and Teacher, have washed your feet, you also should wash one another's feet. I have set you an example that you should do as I have done for you. I tell you the truth, no servant is greater than his master, nor is a messenger greater than the one who sent him. Now that you know these things, you will be blessed if you do them."

In this passage Jesus confirms to the disciples that he is Lord and Teacher. He has also given them an example of God, humble God as servant. Yet, this incredible model of agape love would also be purposeless and unimportant, except as an inspiring illustration of a good person, if we could not confirm that it came from Jesus as God. So the foot washing is like dynamite being lit from a long fuse in one of the old Western movies, one of the Oaters. We watch the fuse in the foot washing, and then the explosion comes in the prophecy following:

> John 13:18-19, NKJV: "I am not referring to all of you; I know those I have chosen. But

this is to fulfill the Scripture: 'He who shares my bread has lifted up his heel against me.' "I am telling you now before it happens, so that when it does happen you will believe that I AM *He*."

Jesus predicts his betrayal by an intimate friend whose feet he washed, Judas, who will lift his heel against him as a wild, rebellious horse might lift his heel against the master who feeds him. Jon Courson explains that, in this passage, Jesus is quoting from:

Psalm 41:9, where the reference is to David's betrayal by a man named Ahithophel. . . . When David's son, Absalom, launched a rebellion against him, Ahithophel, David's key advisor, defected and joined Absalom. . . . What happened to David, though, was simply a picture of what would happen to the Son of David, Jesus Christ, as Jesus would be betrayed by the one who ate bread with Him. . . . And Ahithophel was a picture of what would happen to Judas, for like Judas, he too eventually hanged himself because of guilt (2 Samuel 17:23).[6]

Jesus references this Psalm and boldly proclaims that he will be betrayed by one of the disciples, and further predicts that when this occurs his other disciples will believe that Jesus is I AM because his prophecy came true. In fact, all of his disciples, aside from Judas, did believe Jesus was I AM, a belief for which all of the disciples were martyred except for John.

> **Deuteronomy 18:21-22:** You may say to yourselves, "How can we know when a message has not been spoken by the LORD?" If what a prophet proclaims in the name of the LORD does not take place or come true, that is a message the LORD has not spoken. That prophet has spoken presumptuously. Do not be afraid of him.

Jesus left this prophecy about Judas as an encouragement to the disciples and to us. But it was not just Jesus exercising his prophetic powers, great as they were. It was not just Jesus comforting his disciples about his knowledge and acceptance of his fate. It was not just Jesus declaiming his omniscience or oneness with God, the Father. It was not just Jesus accepting an unfortunate and ill-fated destiny brought on by a traitor. It was God, Jesus, unfolding part of the plan, which would be our redemption. In the end, I AM was say-

week two

> The whole meaning of Christianity rests on the truth of Christ's being who he said he was and accomplishing what he prophesied.

ing that it was God's choice, his appointment and designation to allow this betrayal. Why? Because Jesus is I AM, Messiah and Savior. All his predictions happened, not just generally, but precisely as he uttered them. **That is a message the Lord has spoken.**

Jesus, throughout his ministry, proclaimed that he fulfilled every prophecy spoken of him throughout all of Scripture.

> **Luke 24:25-27:** He said to them, "How foolish you are, and how slow of heart to believe all that the prophets have spoken! Did not the Christ have to suffer these things and then enter his glory?" And beginning with Moses and all the Prophets, he explained to them what was said in all the Scriptures concerning himself.

> **Matthew 5:17-18:** "Do not think that I have come to abolish the Law or the Prophets; I have not come to abolish them but to fulfill them. I tell you the truth, until heaven and earth disappear, not the smallest letter, not the least stroke of a pen, will by any means disappear from the Law until everything is accomplished."

week two

> **Luke 24:44: He said to them, "This is what I told you while I was still with you: Everything must be fulfilled that is written about me in the Law of Moses, the Prophets and the Psalms."**

What a comfort to us that we can intellectually evaluate Jesus' claims that he is I AM. We can see the fulfillment of all of the prophecies spoken about him. Nelson's *Illustrated Bible Dictionary* says:

> *Over 300 prophecies in the Bible speak of Jesus Christ. Specific details given by these prophecies include His tribe (Genesis 49:10), His birthplace (Micah 5:2), dates of His birth and death (Daniel 9:25-26), His forerunner John the Baptist (Malachi 3:1; 4:5; Matthew 11:10), His career and ministry (Isaiah 52:13-53:12), His crucifixion (Psalm 22:1-18), His resurrection (Psalm 16:8-11; Acts 2:25-28), His ascension (Psalm 2; Acts 13:33), and His exaltation as a priest-king (Psalm 110; Acts 2:34).*[7]

Psalm 22 and Isaiah 52 and 53 speak of Jesus' painful death on the cross as an atonement for our sins.

Psalm 22:16-18: Dogs have surrounded me; a band of evil men has encircled me, they have pierced my hands and my feet. I can count all my bones; people stare and gloat over me. They divide my garments among them and cast lots for my clothing.

Isaiah 52:13-14: See, my servant will act wisely; he will be raised and lifted up and highly exalted. Just as there were many who were appalled at him—his appearance was so disfigured beyond that of any man and his form marred beyond human likeness. . . .

Isaiah 53:5: But he was pierced for our transgressions, he was crushed for our iniquities; the punishment that brought us peace was upon him, and by his wounds we are healed.

Today's Exercise
Circle the portion of the above Scripture that is especially meaningful to you today. Why is this Scripture meaningful to you today?

Prayer
Write a prayer in response to the Scriptures you studied today.

Further Revelation
Write down any answers you had to prayer this week. What new revelations did you receive about our Lord? Write down any thoughts you have about this week.

Weekly Exercise
This week we studied and meditated on Jesus as I AM. I AM came to our earthly home in the flesh and suffered a death on the cross so that we might live with him in his heavenly home. Though the cross conjures images of great suffering and injustice to Jesus, it should also represent, to those in Christ, joy, hope, grace, love, and, in essence, a "welcome home" banner. At some point this next week set aside fifteen minutes and sit before a cross in your community. It could be a cross at your own church, a cross in a chapel, a cross on a hill. . . . Intentionally go before the cross and think about all Christ did for humanity and for you individually as he suffered on the cross to pay the price for the sins of the whole world. Think of his beating, humiliation, and his physical and spiritual suffering on the cross. Confess to I AM all of your sins and commit to turning away from them. Then open yourself to the truth that you are totally forgiven, accepted and unconditionally loved and favored by God. Close by reading the passage of Scripture below, and intentionally see yourself as the child of God who was lost but is found.

Jesus, the Word

God watches for us to move toward him, and, when we do, he runs toward us, kisses us, clothes us, and prepares a feast in our honor.

> Luke 15:17-24: When he came to his senses, he (the Prodigal Son) said, "How many of my father's hired men have food to spare, and here I am starving to death! I will set out and go back to my father and say to him: Father, I have sinned against heaven and against you. I am no longer worthy to be called your son; make me like one of your hired men." So he got up and went to his father. But while he was still a long way off, his father saw him and was filled with compassion for him; he ran to his son, threw his arms around him and kissed him. The son said to him, "Father, I have sinned against heaven and against you. I am no longer worthy to be called your son." But the father said to his servants," "Quick! Bring the best robe and put it on him. Put a ring on his finger and sandals on his feet. Bring the fattened

week two

calf and kill it. Let's have a feast and celebrate. For this son of mine was dead and is alive again; he was lost and is found." So they began to celebrate.

Write a prayer response below.

WEEK THREE

JESUS, THE MESSIAH

The woman said, "I know that Messiah" (called Christ) "is coming. When he comes, he will explain everything to us." Then Jesus declared, "I who speak to you am he." John 4:25-26

week three

Day 1

JESUS TELLS US WHO HE IS AND WHO WE ARE IN HIM

Jesus often used "I AM," in the way we do, to tell about himself and his character. I have been thinking about how frequently I use "I am" throughout the day to talk about feelings or some aspect of my character which furthers the aims of the day. I begin many sentences with, "I'm a person who. . . ." I use this to describe my character, and, I think, in some ways, to set boundaries with another person. I'm a person who likes to keep busy, and I always have a full schedule, implying, "Don't impinge on my time. I have important things to do. . . ." My descriptions are not all greedy and self-protective. I am a person who also enjoys her friends and family, loves being married, loves taking time with God. I may have this in reverse order, but there it is.

Jesus, in describing his character with "I AM," always, in some way, talks about his divine nature, or reveals his divinity by his character. He was fully human and fully divine, but his human nature was immediately accessible; his divine nature was mystical and testified to by hearsay, that of the Father. But remember, the Father spoke audibly over Jesus during his baptism saying, "You are my Son, whom I love; with you I am well pleased" (Luke 3:22).

Read John 4:1-42:

1. **Jesus used these words to declare that he was the Christ and Messiah, as in John 4:**

> John 4:25-26: The woman said, "I know that Messiah (called Christ) is coming. When he comes, he will explain everything to us." Then Jesus declared, "I who speak to you am he."

I have often marveled at the "Samaritan woman at the well" story because it is a good deal like my own. Jesus revealed to the woman that he was the Christ (meaning "the anointed one"), but also, in paradox to his preeminence as the Christ, he opened the door to the beautiful, awesome, stunning aspects of his character—his humility, love and grace.

2. **He revealed many aspects of his character to her.** He picked one, maybe the archetype of the lowliest creature on earth, despised and humiliated. He traveled out of his way to choose an unmarried woman who had been with five men and was now living in sin with her significant other; from a race abhorred by the Jews; so ashamed that she went to the well at a time of day, midday, so hot that no one else in town would be there. Like me, as a person in the heart of my addictions, she had entirely given up on herself and given up all hope of redemption. But somewhere deep, deep in her soul, she had heard about and listened to the speculations and promise about a Messiah, and she believed, perhaps not for herself, but that he would explain who he was. He did explain to her, and, "She got it, baby!" She spread the word, becoming the first witness for our Lord, Jesus Christ. Her courageous evangelism brought many a Samaritan to hear the Lord and to believe in him.

So what did Christ illustrate about himself? He showed her that, yes, he was uncondemning, gracious, loving, a Messiah for her:

> John 4:9-10: The Samaritan woman said to him, "You are a Jew and I am a Samaritan woman. How can you ask me for a drink?" (For Jews do not associate with Samaritans.) Jesus answered her, "If you knew the gift of God and who

Jesus, in describing his character with "I AM," always, in some way, talks about his divine nature, or reveals his divinity by his character.

> it is that asks you for a drink, you would have asked him and he would have given you living water."

One could go on and on, rant really, about the character of I AM, his kindness, his tolerance, his patience, his forgiveness, his heart for the broken sinner, his elevation of women, (I personally think Jesus was the first feminist.) But one of the most remarkable traits of Jesus is that he, so often, shows us who we are at our very best. The Samaritan woman found herself, who she truly was, when all the dirt and years of sin dimming her luster were washed clean and restored by living water as a result of one conversation with Jesus.

We, like the Samaritan woman, will be defined by the world, which gladly creates and highlights our every fault and stifles and subdues who we are in Christ. We need to look no further than multibillion dollar cosmetic and diet industries to illustrate this point.

But the beginning of Ephesians is one of many passages that tell of who we are in Christ:

> **Ephesians 1:3-14: Praise be to the God and Father of our Lord Jesus Christ, who has blessed us in the heavenly realms with every spiritual blessing in Christ. For he chose us in him before the cre-**

ation of the world to be holy and blameless in his sight. In love he predestined us to be adopted as his sons through Jesus Christ, in accordance with his pleasure and will—to the praise of his glorious grace, which he has freely given us in the one he loves. In him we have redemption through his blood, the forgiveness of sins, in accordance with the riches of God's grace that he lavished on us with all wisdom and understanding. And he made known to us the mystery of his will according to his good pleasure, which he purposed in Christ, to be put into effect when the times will have reached their fulfillment—to bring all things in heaven and on earth together under one head, even Christ. In him we were also chosen, having been predestined according to the plan of him who works out everything in conformity with the purpose of his will, in order that we, who were the first to hope in Christ, might be for the praise of his glory. And you also were included in Christ when you heard the word of truth, the gospel of your salvation. Having believed, you were marked in him with a seal, the promised Holy Spirit, who is a deposit guaranteeing our inheritance until the redemption of those who are God's possession—to the praise of his glory.

week three

Today's Exercise
Underline every word in this passage which defines who you are in Christ. Review the underlined words. What is most meaningful to you today and why?

Write that word on your hand to remind yourself of it throughout this day.

Prayer
Pray for yourself to let go of being defined by this world, and instead let yourself be defined by who you are in Christ. Pray over specific areas of struggle.

Day 2
THE TESTIMONY OF THE FATHER

Jesus further reveals his character in John 7:28-29 at one of the great celebratory times for the Jews. One of the important feasts of the Jews was the Feast of Tabernacles. They celebrated with great joy, as they were commanded by God the Father, with boisterous shouting and singing every day of the feast. Integral to the Feast of Tabernacles was God's people asking I AM for the Messiah, their Savior. The disciples appealed earnestly to Jesus not to go to the Feast; for whatever reasons, perhaps unbelief that he was truly the Messiah and could perform works and miracles, and preach with authority. Jesus told them his time had not yet come and sent the disciples ahead to the Feast while he remained behind. With all the sense of great story, irony, denouement, and climax, Jesus did go up to the Feast by himself, in secret. He did speak. As ever, his wisdom and logic were spiritually fluent and impeccable.

Much could be said about what he spoke at the Feast of Tabernacles; that he stymied the Jewish scholars with his logic, using their own premises from Mosaic law; that he called to people to think for themselves and not judge according to appearances; that he asked, even adjured people to seek the glory of God the Father, and not their own. Finally, he spoke with authority and called with passion ("cried out" as translated in John 7:28) as the man, as the Messiah, as God.

> John 7:28-29: Then Jesus, still teaching in the temple courts, cried out, "Yes, you know me, and you know where I am from. I am not here on my own, but he who sent me is true. You do not know him, but I know him because I am from him and he sent me."

Jesus often takes the premise of debate given to him by the people to whom he is speaking. In this case, the people are questioning that he is the Messiah, saying that the Messiah is supposed to come in secret. Jesus takes that premise and says, "Yes, you know me and where I am from on earth. OK. OK! But think about this. I'm not here on my own. I am here as an ambassador of God the Father, from heaven."

Adam Clarke, in his commentary on this passage says:

> *Our Lord takes them up on their own profession, and argues from it. Since you have got so much information concerning me, add this to it, to make it complete; namely, that I am not come of myself; am no self-created or self-authorized prophet; I came from God:-the testimony of John the Baptist, the descent of the Holy Spirit, the voice from heaven, the purity and excellence of my doctrine, and the multitude of my miracles, sufficiently attest this. Now, God is true who has borne testimony to me; but ye know him not, therefore it is that this testimony is disregarded.*[1]

Over and over Jesus tells us that he is not a free spirit come to show the way for humanity, as the New Agers would have it. According to the I AM Scripture of John 7:28-29, he was sent by God the Father; he came with a mission, the redemption of humankind; he is part and parcel of the Father; the Father bore testimony, witness to Jesus in every way—this is an unqualified statement. So, whether Jesus was doing miracles or speaking wisdom, or performing any supernatural act, it was on the authority of the Father, who testified to his words and deeds; he came to reveal God to people because they did not understand the character of God the Father and, therefore, did not know him.

Informing the people, and especially the learned and clerics of the day, that Jesus' Father bore testimony, was of utmost importance to Jesus. In Mosaic Law the testimony of two witnesses was required to establish the truth of any claim for or against any person. So again, in John chapter eight, we have the iteration in an I AM statement of the Father's witness.

When I was in Jerusalem studying the Palestine of Jesus, I learned that, in the time of Jesus, men came to the synagogue to debate. The Jews never listened politely to a speaker, nodding their heads and occasionally clapping their approval, as we do today. They challenged, sometimes, every statement made. I was interested, and somewhat amused, that several groups might be gathered in the outer aisles at one time.

This would mean that Jesus might be one of several men talking, proselytizing, debating at the same time. But I am betting that Jesus always drew the largest crowds and the most formidable debaters because of his originality, presumption, intelligence, pointed and often pugnacious wisdom. There is verification of this in John 8:13-20:

> The Pharisees challenged him,
> "Here you are, appearing as

With all the sense of great story, irony, denouement, and climax, Jesus did go up to the Feast by himself, in secret.

your own witness; your testimony is not valid." Jesus answered, "Even if I testify on my own behalf, my testimony is valid, for I know where I came from and where I am going. But you have no idea where I come from or where I am going. You judge by human standards; I pass judgment on no one. But if I do judge, my decisions are right, because I am not alone. I stand with the Father, who sent me. In your own Law it is written that the testimony of two men is valid. I am one who testifies for myself; my other witness is the Father, who sent me."Then they asked him, "Where is your father?" "You do not know me or my Father," Jesus replied. "If you knew me, you would know my Father also."He spoke these words while teaching in the temple area near the place where the offerings were put. Yet no one seized him, because his time had not yet come.

One must make a distinction here between earthly testimony and divine testimony. Jesus could have no earthly witnesses because no human could attest to his claims. They didn't

week three

know where he came from, where he was going, or why he was here. To them, he was one mysterious, inscrutable, if mystical, itinerant preacher who was doing and saying a lot of really astonishing, amazing, even divinely inspired things. But they could not affirm his divinity.

So we learn again about I AM; that God the Father and Jesus are one and yet separate; that their testimony is equal; that they are both divine; that they share equally in authority and truth. I have often thought about the Pharisees and their debates with Jesus. I have frequently wondered if I were there in person and heard Jesus' words, would I believe? Would I instantly and automatically accept the words of Jesus? I know that I would not have debated. I would probably have clapped unenthusiastically; or perhaps not. I might have thought him blasphemous and kept very still. I would have debated within myself, probably not out loud; not because I wouldn't have argued, I would, but because I would be afraid of his answer, afraid of being made a fool. "Vanity, vanity, all is vanity," as Solomon said. I believe I would have fallen by the way, discounted the words of our Savior and sought other easier avenues of spirituality. In fact, I can relate far more to the Pharisees than to those who believed in Jesus when he was here. Imagine telling the world that you are God, that you are equal to God the Father, and that you are here to save everyone who wants to be saved. Well, well it's just way too fantastic to be accepted!

Yet the Holy Spirit testifies to our spirit that

what Jesus said is true and we can, because of him, become a child of God. Romans 8:15-16 tells us, "For you did not receive a spirit that makes you a slave again to fear, but you received the Spirit of sonship. And by him we cry, 'Abba, Father.' The Spirit himself testifies with our spirit that we are God's children."

Today's Exercise
The Word of God reveals that the spirit of fear and a spirit of sonship/daughtership are opposed to each other. For if we truly believe the Father's testimony, that we are his children, then we will not live under a spirit of fear. In the space provided below list things in your life that bring you under a spirit of fear, right now.

Prayer
Lift your fears specifically to the Lord and ask him to give you a spirit of sonship/daughtership and to remove your spirit of fear.

Day 3
FOLLOW ME

When Jesus uses the indirect form of I AM he often tells us who we are in relationship to him and how we disciples should behave.

In John 12:26, Jesus says:

> "Whoever serves me must follow me; and where I am, my servant also will be. My Father will honor the one who serves me."

1. **Jesus commands us to follow him.** This passage reveals several aspects of Christ's character, as well as his expectations from his followers. Christ begins to unfurl the scroll of discipleship. He shows the importance of being a servant, his own character as well as what ours should be. When Christ says that whoever serves him must follow him he is directing, nay commanding, that we must remain open to his instruction, his wisdom, and also to his guidance of our lives. This passage, in addition, means that Jesus will choose, appoint, and stand with us in our ministries; that, as a matter of obedience, we will join

Jesus where he is and where he is performing his works to the benefit of mankind.

In the Bible workbook, *Experiencing God*, the authors, Henry T. Blackaby and Claude V. King, exhort us to join God where he is working.[2]

2. **Jesus will be with us forever.** There is, by implication, an additional promise here that we will be with Jesus forever; that he will take us to be where he is. The time and place are not limited in this Scripture. Once we take Jesus as our Lord and Savior we step over into heavenly time and space, eternity and the presence of God, whether here on earth or in heaven. There is no longer any boundary. Because Jesus went to his Father, the kingdom of Heaven is within us.

3. **Spend time with Jesus.** This passage also carries the idea of the importance of "hanging out with the Master." In one story of Mary and Martha, the sisters of Lazarus, Martha complains to Jesus that she has to do all the work, the cooking, cleaning, serving the food, gathering up, and storing all the leftovers, while Mary just sits around with him listening to and lapping up his words and doing bloody nothing. You would think Jesus would say, "Hey that's right, Martha! I'll get on Mary's case right away. Naughty, naughty, Mary!" But he tells Martha exactly the opposite:

> **Luke 10:40-42:** But Martha was distracted by all the preparations that had to be made. She came to him and

> When Christ says that whoever serves him must follow him, he is directing, nay commanding, that we must remain open to his instruction, his wisdom, and also to his guidance of our lives.

asked, "Lord, don't you care that my sister (Mary) has left me to do the work by myself? Tell her to help me!"

"Martha, Martha," the Lord answered, "you are worried and upset about many things, but only one thing is needed. Mary has chosen what is better, and it will not be taken away from her."

4. Servants of Jesus will be honored. Last, but certainly not least, if we are servants of Jesus we will be honored by the Father. This is a concept I have thought about a lot. I just love the promises of Scripture, and the fact that they will not return void. If our Abba, Daddy in heaven, and our Lord said it, it's true. I think we cannot really even begin to imagine the heavenly, spiritual treasures God has in store for those who love and serve him.

> 1 Corinthians 2:9: "No eye has seen, no ear has heard, no mind has conceived what God has prepared for those who love him."

The idea of being with Jesus eternally is frequently expressed by him with the I AM phraseology:

John 14:3: "And if I go and prepare a place for you, I will come back and take you to be with me that you also may be where I am."

This passage promises that he will make a place for all his followers in a heavenly home, and that he will come again and escort us to the place he has prepared, and then he will be with us, his followers, eternally.

Today's Exercise
John 12:26 uncovered four truths for us today: 1) Jesus commands us to follow him, 2) Jesus will be with us forever 3) We should spend time with Jesus, 4) Servants of Jesus will be honored. What was the most meaningful truth to you today and why?

week three

Prayer
It is so important that we spend time with Jesus. Praying is a wonderful way to spend time with our Lord. At some point during the day set aside ten minutes to pray to Jesus with the intention of just spending time with him and enjoying your relationship with him. Talk with him about anything you want, even your hair color or what you want for dinner. Then spend at least three minutes of your time listening for his gentle voice of love.

Day 4
THE GLORY OF THE SON

Jesus again brings forth more in another indirect I AM saying, which leads us to greater insight into who he is.

> **John 17:24:** "Father, I want (will) those you have given me to be with me where I am, and to see my glory, the glory you have given me because you loved me before the creation of the world."

1. **The Will of Jesus.** These are among the last words spoken before he went to the Garden of Gethsemane. In other Bible versions the "I want" is translated "I will." It carries the idea that Jesus was not just desiring, hoping that his followers would be with him, he was bringing all his authority, divinity, and majesty to bear upon the issue of his disciples, then and now, being with him. In the Jamieson, Fausset and Brown Commentary, it says:

> *Let us attend, first, to the style of petition here only employed by our Lord: "I will." The majesty of this style of speaking is the first thing that strikes the reverential reader. Some good expositors, indeed . . . , conceive that nothing more is meant by this word than a simple wish, desire, request. . . . But such a word from the mouth of a creature cannot determine its sense, when taken up into the lips of the Son of God. Thus, when He said to the leper (Matt 8:3), "I will . . . , be thou clean!" something more, surely, was meant than a mere wish for his recovery.*[3]

Often Jesus says "I want" or "I pray." But here, in this passage, right before his betrayal, the King issues a directive, "I will that those you have given me be with me forever."

2. **The Father gives the Son glory.** Then Jesus steps, rather strides into eternity, divinity, and union with his beloved Father. I am struck and touched by this scriptural passage and what it says about the love between Father and Son. Jesus has no qualms about receiving his own glory because it came from his Father who has always loved him. How many times have I, with false humility, said, "Oh no, no don't thank me. It's not necessary," while secretly enjoying, thoroughly, the praise of people? How

refreshing that Jesus says, "Yes, yes, indeed let my people be with me that they may see my glory, which you gave me because you loved me." Jesus, here, before the Garden of Gethsemane, says nothing of his human nature, and what he says about his earthly journey is entirely couched in terms of the divine nature of him and his Father, and their imperishable, perpetual union. Jamieson, Fausset and Brown describe the glory of Jesus in this way:

> *It is not His essential glory, the glory of His Divine Personality, but His glory as the Incarnate Head of His people, the Second Adam of a redeemed humanity, in which glory the Father beheld Him with ineffable complacency from everlasting. Jesus regards it as glory enough for us to be admitted to see and gaze forever upon this His glory! This is 'the beatific vision;' but it shall be no mere vision—we shall be like Him, for we shall see Him as He is" 1 John 3:2.*[4]

The Father loved Jesus before the foundation of the world and sent Jesus to reconcile us to the Father, so that we might share in their union and their love. As I study the life of Jesus it is a resounding "yes" that Jesus my Lord is glorified and worshiped eternally by all creation. But what is unfathomable is that

week three

Jesus desires to share his glory, so we too may share in the glory of Father and Son. Jesus wills for us to have lives that manifest the Father's beauty, power, honor, holiness, greatness, and authority.

> John 14:12-14: "I tell you the truth, anyone who has faith in me will do what I have been doing. He will do even greater things than these, because I am going to the Father. And I will do whatever you ask in my name, so that the Son may bring glory to the Father. You may ask me for anything in my name, and I will do it."
>
> John 15:8: "This is to my Father's glory, that you bear much fruit, showing yourselves to be my disciples."
>
> John 16:14-15: "He will bring glory to me by taking from what is mine and making it known to you. All that belongs to the Father is mine. That is why I said the Spirit will take from what is mine and make it known to you."
>
> John 17:22-23: "I have given them the glory that you gave

Jesus has no qualms about receiving his own glory because it came from his Father who has always loved him.

me, that they may be one as we are one: I in them and you in me. May they be brought to complete unity to let the world know that you sent me and have loved them even as you have loved me."

week three

Today's Exercise
Of the last four verses you just read, circle the verse that is most meaningful to you today. Why is this verse meaningful to you?

Prayer
Pray for the day ahead of you, that you would live it to glorify Jesus. Ask to be shown how to glorify Jesus this day, and write down any impressions you have as to how you can glorify him today.

Day 5
THE POWER OF HIS NAME

The final I AM Scripture to be discussed for the week is John 18:5-9.

1. **Deliberate embrace of obedience.** Judas led a detachment of troops from the Chief Priests and Pharisees to the Garden of Gethsemane. Jesus did not wait for them to search out or even approach his position. As God he knew why they were there and what his fate would be. His going forward to meet them, an act of courage and deliberate embrace of obedience, said to everyone present, "I am the master of my destiny. Of my free will I go to my death." I contrast this with how often, earlier in his ministry, Jesus avoided capture because the time for his betrayal and death was not ready to be fulfilled. We have already discussed two times when he avoided being seized. At the Feast of Tabernacles, when he argued with the Jews in the temple courts, they attempted to take hold of him.

week three

> John 7:30: At this they tried to seize him, but no one laid a hand on him, because his time had not yet come.

Another example of the people's unsuccessfully trying to seize and kill Jesus is found in John 8:58-59:

> "I tell you the truth," Jesus answered, "before Abraham was born, I AM!" At this, they picked up stones to stone him, but Jesus hid himself, slipping away from the temple grounds.

If ever there were a time for Jesus to do a disappearing act it was in the Garden of Gethsemane, because the detachment of troops was deadly serious. They were bearing torches to clearly see the person to be arrested, and they had weapons. With all the grandeur and loftiness of a king, Jesus took complete command of the situation. He did not lurk in any shadow, nook, or cranny of the garden, of which there must have been many. When I was in Jerusalem, I visited the supposed Garden of Gethsemane, and there was a very old and capacious olive tree, thought not to be as old as the time of Jesus. Of course, I didn't listen to this, but I imagined that he sat by it, perhaps even on it. It was quite large enough to hide behind or in. Yet that was never a consideration for him. "Get thee behind me, Diana

> His going forward to meet them, an act of courage and deliberate embrace of obedience, said to everyone present, "I am the master of my destiny. Of my free will I go to my death."

Satan," he would have said. He then took full possession of his divinity and his fate.

> **John 18:4-6**: Jesus, knowing all that was going to happen to him, went out and asked them, "Who is it you want?" "Jesus of Nazareth," they replied. "I AM he," Jesus said. (And Judas the traitor was standing there with them.) When Jesus said, "I AM he," they drew back and fell to the ground.

2. **Jesus displays his divinity.** The full extent of Jesus' power and divinity was on display here. Of his own free will he went forward; the cortege, seeking him, did not recognize him, which would have offered another means of escape. When they asked, he replied, and complied fully with his destiny and his captors. The mere godly presence of Jesus slew his captors in the Spirit, and they fell backward, affording even another chance for Jesus' escape. When the captors regained their feet and some semblance of order, Jesus asked them again:

> **John 18:7-9**: "Who is it you want?" And they said, "Jesus of Nazareth." "I told you that I AM he," Jesus answered. "If you are looking for me, then let these men go." This hap-

> pened so that the words he had spoken would be fulfilled: "I have not lost one of those you gave me."

Jesus had complete power over his enemies and his friends. He willingly surrendered himself to his enemies while, at the same time, protecting his disciples, his friends, to the last man among them. The fact that Jesus was I AM did not need to be stated directly in the Garden of Gethsemane. His radiance and resplendence, the full majestic voice of eternal love was enough to subdue with overawe, not just a few bystanders and captors in the Garden, but all who were in the presence of God.

At the very sound of his name, the name of I AM, all were prostrate before him. What a visual picture for us of the very power of his name. Listen to what Jesus told his followers about the power of his name.

> John 14:13-14: "And I will do whatever you ask in my name, so that the Son may bring glory to the Father. You may ask me for anything in my name, and I will do it."

> John 15:16-17: "You did not choose me, but I chose you and appointed you to go and bear fruit—fruit that will last. Then the Father will give you

whatever you ask in my name. This is my command: Love each other."

John 16:23-24: "In that day you will no longer ask me anything. I tell you the truth, my Father will give you whatever you ask in my name. Until now you have not asked for anything in my name. Ask and you will receive, and your joy will be complete."

Jesus tells us when we ask anything in his name he will do it. Asking in the name of Jesus is not merely closing each prayer and saying "in the name of Jesus." Rather, asking in the name of Jesus is walking with him in such a way that we are living and praying in complete harmony with who he is.

week three

Today's Exercise
Where are you walking/praying in harmony with the Lord and where are you not? Record your thoughts below.

Prayer
A natural outflow of seeking intimacy with God by deeply studying God's Word is to be able to pray more powerful prayers in the name of Jesus. Where do you need to see God's awesome power in your life? Lift this area of your life to the Father and boldly and specifically ask him for what you desire in the name of Jesus.

Further Revelation
Write down any answers you had to prayer this week. What new revelations did you receive about our Lord? Write down any thoughts you have about this week.

Weekly Exercise

Jesus, throughout his ministry, tells us who he is, but he also tells us who we are in him. This week we learned that, in Christ, we are his children, that we are honored, glorious, and powerful. Additionally, the passage from Ephesians 1 on Day 2 brings forth many aspects of our identity in Christ.

Pick out four or five words that are meaningful to you. Then post them in some thoughtful way that will bring a constant and rather permanent reminder of who you are in Christ. Be creative and have fun with this project.

WEEK FOUR

JESUS, THE BREAD OF LIFE

*Then Jesus declared, "I AM the bread of life.
He who comes to me will never go hungry,
and he who believes in me will never be thirsty."*
John 6:35

week four

Day 1
BREAD – THE STAFF OF LIFE

The third category of I AM sayings in John is called the "allegorical" or "metaphorical" sayings, of which we will discuss seven in the Book of John and several in the Book of Revelation in the next chapters (note that if you have purchased the book in two volumes, some of these will appear in the first volume, and the rest in the second volume).

The first saying is when Jesus declares himself to be the bread of life. I, Diana, started a novel about a first century woman in Rome, who, among other talents, could bake bread. In the time of Jesus, Paul, and Nero, wonderful breads of many flavors existed; herb, olive, cinnamon and raisin, and all could be drizzled with olive oil and honey. Bread was not only the staff of life but the pleasure of gourmands and gourmets alike.

My own grandmother was a great cook. She could do everything from making oxtail soup to canning apples for the best applesauce I ever ate. I don't remember her ever baking bread. It doesn't mean she didn't bake bread; I just don't remember it. So I asked my husband. He remembers very well his grandmother baking bread, kneading the dough like washing and scrubbing laundry (like women kneading their clothes on the rocks of the rivers in olden times); shaping them into loaves, gentle appealing curves; putting them in the oven, and he recalls the aroma and the steamy glisten of the crust when it came out of the oven. He'd spread some butter and savor every bite. That was when bread was bread and not dinero and dollars! It must have been something like what people from earliest biblical times experienced in the baking and eating of bread.

Bread in the Old Testament

Bread always played an important, even a crucial, part in the lives of people in the Old Testament. Abraham made a meal of freshly made bread and meat for the angels, who told him he would have a child in the next year. Esau sold his birthright for a meal of stew and savory bread, which Jacob also gave to his father, in order to steal Esau's birthright.

> **Genesis 25:34: Then Jacob gave Esau some bread and some lentil stew. He ate and drank,**

and then got up and left. So Esau despised his birthright.

Joseph, steward of the King's supplies in a time of drought, sent his brothers home to their father, Jacob, with large amounts of grain to make bread. God fed the Israelites with manna in the wilderness and commanded his people to bring bread offerings and to always keep bread before him in the tabernacle.

Abigail, the wife of a king who mistreated David, saved her husband by bringing food including some two hundred loaves of bread (1 Samuel 25:18). Isaiah invites all who are spiritually hungry and thirsty to come and feast for free on the Lord and his wisdom (Isaiah 55:1-2).

Much can be learned about our Lord by studying the story of David and his starving men eating the holy bread of the Presence.

> David went to Nob, to Ahimelech the priest. Ahimelech trembled when he met him, and asked, "Why are you alone? Why is no one with you?" David answered Ahimelech the priest, "The king charged me with a certain matter and said to me, 'No one is to know anything about your mission and your instructions.' As for my men, I have told them to meet me at a certain place. Now then, what do you have on

Jesus knows our deepest spiritual needs but also understands and even celebrates our humanness. We get hungry, and bread certainly does taste good.

hand? Give me five loaves of bread, or whatever you can find." But the priest answered David, "I don't have any ordinary bread on hand; however, there is some consecrated bread here—provided the men have kept themselves from women." David replied, "Indeed women have been kept from us, as usual whenever I set out. The men's things are holy even on missions that are not holy. How much more so today!" So the priest gave him the consecrated bread, since there was no bread there except the bread of the Presence that had been removed from before the LORD and replaced by hot bread on the day it was taken away (1 Samuel 21:1-6).

Jesus used this story to strongly caution the Pharisees against their legalism and lack of compassion.

Matthew 12:3-8: He answered, "Haven't you read what David did when he and his companions were hungry? He entered the house of God, and he and his companions ate the consecrated bread—which was not

> lawful for them to do, but only for the priests. Or haven't you read in the Law that on the Sabbath the priests in the temple desecrate the day and yet are innocent? I tell you that one greater than the temple is here. If you had known what these words mean, 'I desire mercy, not sacrifice,' you would not have condemned the innocent. For the Son of Man is Lord of the Sabbath."

Jesus knows our deepest spiritual needs but also understands and even celebrates our humanness. We get hungry, and bread certainly does taste good. We get tired, and a day of rest is quite wonderful. Our Lord has compassion on our very human estate and wants to pour out his loving kindness on every part of our lives, right down to the very bread we enjoy.

> Luke 12:27-31: "Consider how the lilies grow. They do not labor or spin. Yet I tell you, not even Solomon in all his splendor was dressed like one of these. If that is how God clothes the grass of the field, which is here today, and tomorrow is thrown into the fire, how much more will he clothe you, O you of little faith! And

do not set your heart on what you will eat or drink; do not worry about it. For the pagan world runs after all such things, and your Father knows that you need them. But seek his kingdom, and these things will be given to you as well."

week four

Today's Exercise
Jesus tells us not to worry because God will take care of us in grand style the way he takes care of the lilies of the field. He tells us instead to seek the kingdom of God—meaning that, instead of worrying, trust Jesus' solutions, his character, his entire reign over our lives. Instead of worrying, how can you seek Jesus and the kingdom of heaven in the day ahead of you?

Prayer
Bring Jesus all the worries that may plague you this week. Ask Jesus to intervene with each worry and teach you how, instead, to focus on him. Think over the tasks you have ahead of you today. What practical help do you need from the Lord in your day? Ask the Lord for his very practical help. What would bring you joy? Ask for that, too.

Day 2
OLD TESTAMENT SNAPSHOTS OF JESUS

A wonderful revelation of Jesus as I AM is that he always draws the prayer shawl of the Old Testament over his shoulders as he explains to us about who he is and how he fulfills every prophesy of the Messiah and completes, in every regard, the predicate of I AM. Jesus planned everything, down to the minutest detail, including the timing of allegorical sayings. Can you guess? Of course, when Jesus uttered the bread of life sayings the feast was Passover, "the Pasch of the Jews," as it was called by the Jews.

The Passover Feast

John 6:4: Now the Passover, a feast of the Jews was near.

The Pasch of the Jews was connected, annexed also to the "Feast of Unleavened Bread." The Feast of Unleavened Bread and the Passover Feast commemorated the time in which the Lord brought the Israelites out of Egypt. He saved them from a life of slavery and death. God had been telling Pharaoh, time and again, to let his people go. But Pharaoh, whose heart was hardened, would not.

Finally, after a number of plagues brought by the Lord, which did not loosen the bricks around Pharaoh's heart, the Lord told Moses he was going to kill all the firstborn of Egypt. The Jews would be saved by substituting the blood of lambs for their own. God instructed them to slaughter male lambs without defect at twilight and place the blood of spotless lambs upon the sides and the tops of their doorframes (Exodus 12: 5-11).

All the houses with blood on the doors would be passed over, and the firstborn in those houses saved. Quite elaborate procedures were set up by God to signify the separation of the Israelites from the Egyptians, both physically and spiritually. The Passover sealed a time of grace and salvation for a people chosen by God. Jesus is our Passover and the bread of the New Covenant.

> *Jesus is both God and man; he declares himself to be our salvation from which we may eat and not die; he is living bread,*

1 Corinthians 5:7-8: For Christ, our Passover lamb, has been sacrificed. Therefore let us keep the Festival (Passover and Unleavened Bread). . . .

Of course, much could be said about Jesus as our Passover lamb; that he was innocent and pure; that he was in his prime; that he was gentle and loving like a lamb to the end; that the blood from his hands, feet, and head matched that of the blood on the doorframes of the Israelites on the night of the Passover. God's wrath would pass over and preserve from death all who were under the protection of the blood of the lamb. The way in which Christ died does not just parallel the Old Testament Passover, it walks exactly in its footsteps, leaving not a jot of dust beside. He was God the Father's perfect sacrifice, the lamb without blemish, to atone for the sins of all if they choose, and to open the way to reconcile all people to himself if they choose.

Wandering in the Wilderness

When the Israelites were in the wilderness, wandering around because they had grumbled and complained against God, did he desert them? Not for a single eternal second! He took care of them in every respect, including their food, water, shelter, and rules to live by in community. I often hear the wilderness referred to as a bad experience that we go through, even today, when we grumble or are disobedient to the Lord. My granddaughter, Mandy, when she was younger and underwent unpleasant experiences, would say, "That was brutal!" She may have learned that expression from my grandson, her older brother, Bradley. That might have been the thinking of the Israelites in the wilderness.

I take a different view. Imagine having the Lord with you every second, taking not just care, but solicitous, mother-hen care of your every need. The Lord rained down bread from heaven, manna, for the people to eat, along with their supernaturally produced quail. OK, we ought to be mindful that this bread rotted and needed to be replenished daily. Our "bread of life," Jesus, is an eternal banquet where we may feed forever without a single hunger pang. Jesus taught us several things about the bread of heaven.

> **John 6:33: "For the bread of God is he who comes down from heaven and gives life to the world."**
>
> **John 6:35: Then Jesus declared, "I AM the bread of life. He who comes to me will never go hungry, and he who believes in me will never be thirsty."**

meaning he not only gives us life after our bodies perish, but he gives life today.

Jesus, the Bread of Life

John 6:47-51: "I tell you the truth, he who believes has everlasting life. I AM the bread of life. Your forefathers ate the manna in the desert, yet they died. But here is the bread that comes down from heaven, which a man may eat and not die. I am the living bread that came down from heaven. If anyone eats of this bread, he will live forever. This bread is my flesh, which I will give for the life of the world."

Jesus says a number of things about his divinity in these passages. He came down from heaven, and is only an earthly creature by choice, in order to bring us salvation. He is both God and man; he declares himself to be our salvation from which we may eat and not die; he is living bread, meaning he not only gives us life after our bodies perish, but he gives life today. He equates the food of bread to his flesh, his body, which will be the perfect sacrifice for all humanity and will satisfy us from hunger. He is the fuel, the inspiration, and the sustenance for our daily lives.

Today's Exercise
Jesus tells us that he is the bread of life and whoever comes to him will never go hungry. What do you hunger for today? What are your deepest needs?

Prayer
Bring every area of hunger to Jesus and ask him to satisfy each area. Sit, bask in, and eat in the presence of the bread of life.

Day 3
GENEROSITY OVERFLOWING

Feeding of the Five Thousand

Many Jews, perhaps all Jews, would have been familiar with the Old Testament stories of the Passover and manna rained down by God. As they came to listen to Jesus during the time of the Passover, their religious upbringing, the context of their traditions, the Passover Feast and the Feast of Unleavened Bread, would certainly have given them "ears to hear" what Jesus was saying. Many grumbled, just as their forefathers in the wilderness, and many complained about Jesus' proclamation that he was the bread of heaven, among other messianic claims, especially the Pharisees, Sadducees, and church elders.

Word had, although, spread that Jesus was healing the sick (John 6:2). So, one day, as Jesus was sitting and talking with his disciples on the mountain, a "multitude" came to hear him. It would be as if a large group, thousands of fans, were coming to hear a rock concert

week four

without food, wine, or even any Evian. Near our home in Colorado is a place called Red Rocks, a beautiful outdoor, natural amphitheater which has played host to many a concert. People often come hours ahead to get good seating, and they bring picnics, drinks and snacks to tide them over through the concert. Yes, I've done it myself.

But here came this multitude to hear Jesus speak with no provision for sustenance whatsoever. Jesus again had provided the perfect setting and time for his signs and his oratory; a time near Passover when people would be hungry without food available. So first Jesus would perform the sign, which both attested to and manifested his godhood. Then he would explain it.

> **John 6:5-6:** When Jesus looked up and saw a great crowd coming toward him, he said to Philip, "Where shall we buy bread for these people to eat?" He asked this only to test him, for he already had in mind what he was going to do.

The people and his disciples expected healing miracles from Jesus, but Jesus would take this opportunity to broaden their horizons as to his omnipotence. We know that, in the Old Testament, in the wilderness, God rained down manna from heaven. In this story, God, Jesus gave them food, fed five thousand from two

Jesus, the Bread of Life

fishes and five barley loaves. He did a sign, a wonder which God the Father had previously done in the wilderness and which only God could do, truly create something from heaven, from nothing or almost nothing. It was a sign that could not help but evoke, in the minds of his audience, the wilderness experience of their forebears with the raining down of manna from heaven.

> John 6:7-13: Philip answered him, "Eight months' wages would not buy enough bread for each one to have a bite!" Another of his disciples, Andrew, Simon Peter's brother, spoke up, "Here is a boy with five small barley loaves and two small fish, but how far will they go among so many?" Jesus said, "Have the people sit down." There was plenty of grass in that place, and the men sat down, about five thousand of them. Jesus then took the loaves, gave thanks, and distributed to those who were seated as much as they wanted. He did the same with the fish. When they had all had enough to eat, he said to his disciples, "Gather the pieces that are left over. Let nothing be wasted." So they

gathered them and filled twelve baskets with the pieces of the five barley loaves left over by those who had eaten.

This passage says so much about the character of I AM, Jesus.
1) he is sufficient for all our needs;
2) he will satisfy all who come to him;
3) his generosity is overflowing, at least twelve baskets full left over;
4) gratitude activates heavenly omnipotence;
5) our part, our willingness to give, in the works of God is important to I AM, no matter how small, even just two fishes and five rolls;
6) he serves all the people bountifully and never puts a restriction on how much they can eat;
7) God is filled with love and compassion for those who seek him.

> John 14:12: "I tell you the truth, anyone who has faith in me will do what I have been doing. He will do even greater things than these, because I am going to the Father."

Many years ago a pastor friend of mine and several others from his church took food to help some people in a disaster area in Mexico. They thought they were taking plenty of grain,

So first Jesus would perform the sign, which both attested to and manifested his godhood. Then he would explain it.

potatoes, rice, etc. On the day of distribution they peered out the window and realized they would never be able to feed the hundreds who had come for food. So the pastor gave thanks before he began to distribute. He did not particularly have in mind the feeding of the five thousand as he began the distribution. As the day wore on his heart soared. Every time he reached into a sack, the amount he needed for the next person or family was always there. At the end of the day they had not had to turn a single person away, and there was still food left over. Somewhere in the day, he had made the connection that God was performing the miracle of the fishes and the loaves.

Dennis Bennett, in his book, *Nine O'clock in the Morning*, tells a story about his wife, Rita, being told that she needed to serve dinner to a large unexpected number of people who had been invited a short time before she removed her casserole from the oven. She was cognizant of the fishes and the loaves, and she too gave thanks and served all the people bountifully with some left over.

week four

Today's Exercise

The feeding of the five thousand revealed seven truths regarding Jesus' character:

1) he is sufficient for all our needs;
2) he will satisfy all who come to him;
3) his generosity is overflowing, at least twelve baskets full left over;
4) gratitude makes a way to activation of heavenly omnipotence;
5) our part, our willingness to give, in the works of God is important to I AM, no matter how small, even just two fish and five rolls;
6) he serves all the people bountifully and never puts a restriction on how much they can eat;
7) God is filled with love and compassion for those who seek him.

Which truth is most meaningful to you today and why?

Jesus, the Bread of Life

Prayer
Gratitude invites the hand of God to work powerfully in our lives. The Psalms exhort us to enter his courts with thanksgiving, to give him praise. Write a prayer of thanksgiving, praising God for who he is and how he has blessed you.

week four

Day 4
BELIEVE IN HIM

The Other Side of the Lake

So, Jesus has now set the stage to explain the miracle he has just performed. He has piqued the curiosity and immersed the people into the depth and abyss of his godhood. John, who writes in a "you are there" style, gives us a sense of what it must have been like to fall under God's wonderful, fascinating attractiveness (like a magnet).

Jesus leaves! We have an amazing storm scene, and then Jesus is on the other side of the lake. When the crowd discovers he's gone, they quickly come to seek him. I have written this part in the present tense to give the immediacy to what the people, the crowd, and the disciples were experiencing with Jesus.

> John 6:24: Once the crowd realized that neither Jesus nor his disciples were there, they got into the boats and went to Capernaum in search of Jesus.

In Jesus' disputation to the crowd, on the

other side of the lake, the great carpenter builds brick by brick to the final incontrovertible conclusion, the house which will never be damaged by any freak of nature.

> **John 6:25-26: When they found him on the other side of the lake, they asked him, "Rabbi, when did you get here?" Jesus answered, "I tell you the truth, you are looking for me, not because you saw miraculous signs but because you ate the loaves and had your fill. . . ."**

Jesus has now told the crowd, "Hey, come on. You're not here because of miracles; you're here because I fed you. Eating, earthly sustenance, that's what is important to you!"

How true this is for me. Earthly sustenance, in the form of money, is what satisfies me. I have often loved, and still do, the almighty buck, bread as dollars, and I have followed whatever and whoever can provide it. Jesus knows my character, exactly the same as that of the multitude.

Then Jesus, having demonstrated the crowd's character (that's us), shows them (us) their incontestable weakness, which cannot be denied. He then reveals the true spiritual sustenance for our lives; the food that endures to eternal life:

Jesus gored the crowd on the true horns of a dilemma— a choice between two equally unfavorable options. They must either believe that this man is who he says he is, the Messiah,

> **John 6:27:** "Do not work for food that spoils, but for food that endures to eternal life, which the Son of Man will give you. On him God the Father has placed his seal of approval."

They ask what they must do to do the works of God. Jesus unveils the astonishing, provocative truth—that they must believe in him; that is their work.

They say that Moses gave their forefathers manna from heaven:

> **John 6:28-33:** Then they asked him, "What must we do to do the works God requires?" Jesus answered, "The work of God is this: to believe in the one he has sent." So they asked him, "What miraculous sign then will you give that we may see it and believe you? What will you do? Our forefathers ate the manna in the desert; as it is written: 'He gave them bread from heaven to eat.'" Jesus said to them, "I tell you the truth, it is not Moses who has given you the bread from heaven, but it is my Father who gives you the true bread from heaven. For the bread of God is he who comes down from heaven and gives life to the world."

or they must go home in the same wretched questioning, unbelieving, and hopeless position in which they came.

Jesus, the Bread of Life

And now Jesus moves in for the proverbial, debater's kill. He leads them to the inevitable desire and prayer of their hearts, the prayer of all our hearts, "Give us a messiah. GIVE US THE MESSIAH. Give us that person who gives life to the world. Bring him here!"

> **John 6:34-35:** "Sir," they said, "from now on give us this bread." Then Jesus declared, "I AM the bread of life. He who comes to me will never go hungry, and he who believes in me will never be thirsty."

He has gored the crowd on the true horns of a dilemma. A dilemma is defined as a choice between two equally unfavorable options. They must either believe that this man is who he says he is, the Messiah, or they must go home in the same wretched questioning, unbelieving, and hopeless position in which they came. Everyone begins to quarrel among themselves, even the disciples. Wouldn't it be wonderful to think that all listeners and disciples resolved the issue by turning to the bread of life, Jesus? Of course, as ever, this is not the case. Even though Jesus tells them that the bread from heaven will produce eternal life:

> **John 6:58:** "This is the bread that came down from heaven. Your forefathers ate manna and died, but he who feeds on

> this bread (Jesus) will live forever."

Many of the disciples found this hard to believe and turned away.

> John 6:66: From this time many of his disciples turned back and no longer followed him.

I have always felt a kinship with Peter. After the disciples left, Jesus turned to the twelve, the handpicked twelve and asked in John 6:67, "Do you also want to go away?" Simon Peter answers with almost sardonic humor and slightly self-pitying faith as would I, "You know there aren't a lot of places for me to go, back to drinking and drugging. Ugh! Besides I do (under my breath I utter 'unfortunately') I do believe."

> John 6:68-69: Simon Peter answered him, "Lord, to whom shall we go? You have the words of eternal life. We believe and know that you are the Holy One of God."

Today's Exercise
Jesus tells the crowd that, "The work of God is this: to believe in the one he has sent" (John 6:29). Yesterday you asked God to satisfy your hungers and needs. Today, take in the reality that your work is to believe that Jesus is the one who fulfills your hungers and needs no matter how big or small. It is not your work to come up with your own solutions, to try to satisfy your own hungers and needs. It is Jesus' work. Journal about how this truth impacts you.

Prayer
We all at times lack belief. But we can pray like the father asking Jesus to heal his son, "Help me overcome my unbelief!" (Mark 9:24). Jesus helps and encourages us in our work of believing with this profound and thrilling truth: "I tell you the truth, if you have faith as small as a mustard seed, you can say to this mountain, 'Move from here to there' and it will move. Nothing will be impossible for you" (Matthew 17:20).

Pray for this faith to believe that Jesus is the bread of life who will satisfy every hunger and every need.

Day 5
THE COMMUNION TABLE

The Tabernacle

After the first Passover in Egypt, the Israelites escaped from their life of slavery, crossed the Red Sea and began their journey in the wilderness. God led the Israelites through the wilderness for a period of time, preparing them to live freely in the Promised Land. While on Mount Sinai Moses received the Ten Commandments and also the instruction to "make a sanctuary for me, and I will dwell among them. Make this tabernacle and all its furnishings exactly like the pattern I will show you" (Exodus 25:8-9). Hebrews tells us that this tabernacle was a copy and a shadow of what was in heaven, hence God's mandate that the tabernacle be made in the exact pattern shown to Moses (Hebrews 8:4-6).

Bread played a vital role in the day to day

routines of the people and the priests of the Tabernacle. God commanded Moses to make a table upon which the bread of the Presence would be set before the Lord at all times. This bread, highly symbolic of God's people, was comprised of twelve loaves indicating directly the twelve tribes of Israel. The priests were commanded to eat this bread each week at the table. The Israelites in gratitude and dedication to God would also bring uncooked and cooked grain offerings, which would be eaten by the Priests. A memorial portion was always burned on the brazen altar in memory of God's provision and his covenant with his people.

The Last Supper

Mark 14:12-16: On the first day of the Feast of Unleavened Bread, when it was customary to sacrifice the Passover lamb, Jesus' disciples asked him, "Where do you want us to go and make preparations for you to eat the Passover?" So he sent two of his disciples, telling them, "Go into the city, and a man carrying a jar of water will meet you. Follow him. Say to the owner of the house he enters, 'The Teacher asks: Where is my guest room,

> Oh how our Lord loves a shared meal. In fact, while he walked this earth, he shared so many meals, even with sinners and the disreputable,

where I may eat the Passover with my disciples?' He will show you a large upper room, furnished and ready. Make preparations for us there." The disciples left, went into the city and found things just as Jesus had told them. So they prepared the Passover.

1 Corinthians 11:23-26 (NKJV): . . . the Lord Jesus on the *same* night in which He was betrayed took bread; and when He had given thanks, He broke *it* and said, "Take, eat; this is My body which is broken for you; do this in remembrance of Me." In the same manner *He* also took the cup after supper, saying, "This cup is the new covenant in My blood. This do, as often as you drink *it*, in remembrance of Me."

We can learn so much about Jesus from these passages. Oh how our Lord loves a shared meal. In fact, while he walked this earth, he shared so many meals, even with sinners and the disreputable, that he was criticized by his enemies who accused him of being a glutton (Matthew 11:19). Of the many things Jesus could have asked us to do to remember him—go on a pilgrimage, fast for three days before a cross, build a temple, serve the poor—instead he simply asks that we share a meal, that we have communion with him and each other, remembering his body and blood. The heart of Jesus is enjoying fellowship, rich, deep, so deep and intimate that he lives within us in perpetual fellowship. Now that is mind blowing!

> John 14:18-20: "I will not leave you as orphans; I will come to you. Before long, the world will not see me anymore, but you will see me. Because I live, you also will live. On that day you will realize that I am in my Father, and you are in me, and I am in you."

The riches of Jesus as the Bread of life are mined by him in the closest union possible between his followers and him. I have always disagreed with fellow Christians about the story of Dracula. They argue the story is straight from the dark side, Satan himself, and glorifies an obscene and grotesque counter to the eternal life offered by Jesus. I think Bram Stoker never portrayed Dracula as anything but total evil incarnate whose only nemesis was Jesus and the Cross of Christ. In one movie about vampires, the people, threatened by the vampires, turn a windmill into a cross which defeats the army of vampires then and there. I think, in some ways, Dracula understood the meaning of the Cross better than some Christians.

that he was criticized by his enemies who accused him of being a glutton.

Jesus, the Bread of Life

In another play about Dracula, he asks a Christian, "Do you not drink the blood and eat the flesh of the one you love?" The answer is, "Yes and yes and yes." Why do we do this? Because Jesus told us to. The priest says variations on these words, in the Episcopal service, when he gives the wafer or the bread, "The Body of Christ, the bread of heaven." And when he gives the wine, he says, "The Blood of Christ, the cup of salvation." In the Eucharistic rite we consume each other. We eat the flesh of Jesus, and he consumes us with the fire of his love and the gift of eternal life. Read again John 6:51-58.

> **John 6:51-58:** "I AM the living bread that came down from heaven. If anyone eats of this bread, he will live forever. This bread is my flesh, which I will give for the life of the world." Then the Jews began to argue sharply among themselves, "How can this man give us his flesh to eat?" Jesus said to them, "I tell you the truth, unless you eat the flesh of the Son of Man and drink his blood, you have no life in you. Whoever eats my flesh and drinks my blood has eternal life, and I will raise him up at the last day. For my flesh is real food and my blood is real

week four

drink. Whoever eats my flesh and drinks my blood remains in me, and I in him. Just as the living Father sent me and I live because of the Father, so the one who feeds on me will live because of me. This is the bread that came down from heaven. Your forefathers ate manna and died, but he who feeds on this bread will live forever."

Today's Exercise
What was the most meaningful part of today's lesson to you and why?

Prayer
Write a prayer in response to what was meaningful to you today and ask the Lord if there is anything he wants you to do in response.

Further Revelation
Write down any answers you had to prayer this week. What new revelations did you receive about our Lord? Write down any thoughts you have about this week.

week four

Weekly Exercise
Bake some bread or buy some at a favorite bakery. It can be quick bread right out of the box or a more complicated recipe. Have fun and enjoy the Lord's presence while you are cooking or picking out at your bakery. Then share the bread with a person or persons whom you love. Invite the Lord to share in the banquet.

WEEK FIVE

JESUS, THE LIGHT OF THE WORLD

When Jesus spoke again to the people, he said, "I AM the light of the world. Whoever follows me will never walk in darkness, but will have the light of life." John 8:12

week five

Day 1

LIGHT AND DARK

As an alcoholic I loved nothing more than the night and the dark side. I chose it to the exclusion of my husband and even my daughter, who was the light of my life. I defended my drinking against everything; I spent intimate time with it more than any person; I took every occasion I could to be with it; I would go with it wherever it led, even to betrayal and death. I was passionately in love with alcohol.

In Charles Dickens' *Oliver Twist,* Bill Sikes is the embodiment of evil. He is a thief, a kidnapper, a sadist, and a murderer, but Nancy loves him. She has a lot of goodness in her. So she returns Oliver to his adoptive home. She returns him from being kidnapped by Bill and from leading life as a thief. She saves him but won't leave Bill Sikes. In the end Bill kills her, brutally beating her to death. I had the same relationship with alcohol as Nancy had with Bill.

> John 3:19: This is the verdict: Light has come into the world, but men loved darkness in-

stead of light because their deeds were evil.

Jesus saved me. He shined his light into my dark heart, and I found his incandescence irresistible. Without him I would be dead today, swallowed by darkness; and, to be honest, it would not have been much of a loss.

From the incipience of creation, God separated light from dark:

> Genesis 1:3-5: And God said, "Let there be light," and there was light. God saw that the light was good, and he separated the light from the darkness. God called the light "day," and the darkness he called "night." And there was evening, and there was morning—the first day.

1. **Light is Crucial in Humanity's Being Able to Function.** On the very first day God created light. It is absolutely the most crucial factor in humanity's being able to function. When I think of a world of complete blackness, black hole blackness, I think of hell and the Prince of Darkness, Satan. If we lived in blackness, in night, we would be reduced to a desiccated powder, or back to dust in no time. We could do nothing.

Plato, the Greek philosopher, wrote about people sitting in a cave who did nothing but watch shadows on the opposite cave wall. Granted this condition was metaphorical for humanity's spiritual and mental darkness, but it would be actual for all mankind if there were no light. We probably would not even see shadows. But God not only created the light, he made it much stronger, more utilitarian and beneficial to man than the dark, which seems to have, as its most utile characteristic, that we can sleep much easier at night and make a good deal more mischief, or, at least, in my case, that was true. Even the light he gave to night, the moon, is far inferior to the sun.

2. **Light is Good.** When God saw that the light was good we now know the extent that the spiritual and metaphorical meaning of light plays. First, the power, the perfection of the light of the sun makes possible all the works of humanity, both for us, our own glory and God's glory; second, it parallels, reminds and prompts by constant repetition, the power and perfection of God the Father and Son; third, God spoke the light into being, and Jesus is the Word. Revelation speaks of the New Jerusalem coming down from heaven, and there will no longer be the sun and the moon,

> Revelation 21:23-24: . . . for the glory of God gives it light, and the Lamb is its lamp. The nations will walk by its light, and the kings of the earth will bring their splendor into it. (See also Revelation 22:5).

Jesus, the Light of the World

> Jesus saved me. He shined his light into my dark heart, and I found his incandescence irresistible.

So Jesus, as the Word, produced the light of the sun and is the light of God and hence the foremost reason the light is good.

3. **God Divided Light and Dark.** It is important to realize that God divided light and dark. They have no part in each other, but here on earth they exist side by side; spiritually and mentally they commingle and often fuse within us. We travel between the worlds of dark and light with complete freedom and ease. The Lord, when he created light and dark, clearly had in mind the good of humanity, not the good of heavenly creatures, who live in everlasting light, but human creatures who would need to know both the light and the dark, be able to move between them, and eventually spiritually to be able to choose between them. Matthew Henry, in his commentary, says:

> *God has thus divided time between light and darkness, because he would daily remind us that this is a world of mixtures and changes. In heaven there is perfect and perpetual light, and no darkness at all; in hell, utter darkness, and no gleam of light. In that world between these two there is a great gulf fixed; but, in this world, they are counterchanged, and we pass daily from one to another, that we may learn to expect the like vicissitudes in the providence of God, peace and*

> *trouble, joy and sorrow, and may set the one over-against the other, accommodating ourselves to both as we do to the light and darkness, bidding both welcome, and making the best of both.*[1]

The apostles Paul, Peter, and John all exhort us to choose the light and reject the darkness.

> **Ephesians 5:8-11:** For you were once darkness, but now you are light in the Lord. Live as children of light (for the fruit of the light consists in all goodness, righteousness and truth) and find out what pleases the Lord. Have nothing to do with the fruitless deeds of darkness, but rather expose them.

> **1 Peter 2:9-11:** But you are a chosen people, a royal priesthood, a holy nation, a people belonging to God, that you may declare the praises of him who called you out of darkness into his wonderful light. Once you were not a people, but now you are the people of God; once you had not received mercy, but now you have received mercy. Dear

friends, I urge you, as aliens and strangers in the world, to abstain from sinful desires, which war against your soul.

1 John 2:9-11: Anyone who claims to be in the light but hates his brother is still in the darkness. Whoever loves his brother lives in the light, and there is nothing in him to make him stumble. But whoever hates his brother is in the darkness and walks around in the darkness; he does not know where he is going, because the darkness has blinded him.

week five

Today's Exercise
Review the verses regarding choosing the light instead of the dark. What was the most meaningful verse to you and why?

Prayer
Write a prayer in response to what was meaningful to you today and ask the Lord if there is anything he wants you to do in response.

Day 2
The Revelation of God as Light in the Old Testament

Throughout biblical history, God's light and appearance to men includes:

- the burning bush that awed and sent forth Moses,
- a pillar of fire that confounded an Egyptian army,
- an awesome and fearsome consuming fire on Mt. Sinai that gave the law,
- a lamp stand that illuminated the Ark of the Covenant,

- a warm metaphorical lamp that guides our feet: "You are my lamp, O LORD; the LORD turns my darkness into light" (2 Samuel 22:29),
- an everlasting light more brilliant than the sun:

> **Isaiah 60:19-21:** The sun will no more be your light by day, nor will the brightness of the moon shine on you, for the LORD will be your everlasting light, and your God will be your glory. Your sun will never set again, and your moon will wane no more; the LORD will be your everlasting light, and your days of sorrow will end. Then will all your people be righteous and they will possess the land forever.

The nature of God, like light, is vast, awesome, terrifying, and explosive but it is also inviting, warm, and soft giving light and warmth to our lives. Moses' relationship with God gives great illumination to this perceived paradox about the nature of God. Though God's hand was always on Moses, Moses' first awareness of I AM came in the form of a burning bush:

> **Exodus 3:1-10:** Now Moses was tending the flock of Jethro his father-in-law, the priest of

Midian, and he led the flock to the far side of the desert and came to Horeb, the mountain of God. There the angel of the LORD appeared to him in flames of fire from within a bush. Moses saw that though the bush was on fire it did not burn up. So Moses thought, "I will go over and see this strange sight—why the bush does not burn up." When the LORD saw that he had gone over to look, God called to him from within the bush, "Moses! Moses!" And Moses said, "Here I am." "Do not come any closer," God said. "Take off your sandals, for the place where you are standing is holy ground." Then he said, "I am the God of your father, the God of Abraham, the God of Isaac and the God of Jacob." At this, Moses hid his face, because he was afraid to look at God.

Moses literally hid his face because he was so afraid of the presence of God. In response to I AM, Moses obediently went to Egypt only to encounter the many wonders of God throughout God's ultimate deliverance of the Israelites by means of the Passover. God made himself manifest to Moses and all the Israelites

week five

as a Pillar of Cloud by day and a Pillar of Fire by night in order to lead his people out of Egypt (see Exodus 14:19-20). Amazing, isn't it, that the pillar of fire brought darkness to one side and light to the other in order to protect the Israelites from the Egyptians until they crossed the Red Sea (see Exodus 14:24-31).

After a short period of time God led the Israelites to Mount Sinai to give the law to the Israelites and to give them instructions for the construction of the Tabernacle as the center of worship. It was God's intent to communicate directly with the Israelites but, like Moses at the burning bush, they were terrified when God spoke directly with them. However, Moses, by the time of his ascension of Mount Sinai, in contrast to his former self, understood the importance and the honor of drawing close to I AM, and so he led the Israelites out to meet him. Can you imagine being able to go out of your house and meet with the living God? I believe I would have been terrified, but I think I would have gone. Would you?

> Exodus 19:16-19: On the morning of the third day there was thunder and lightning, with a thick cloud over the mountain, and a very loud trumpet blast. Everyone in the camp trembled. Then Moses led the people out of the camp to meet with God, and they stood at the foot of the mountain. Mount Sinai was

The nature of God, like light, is vast, awesome, terrifying, and explosive but it is also inviting, warm, and soft giving light and warmth to our lives.

covered with smoke, because the LORD descended on it in fire. The smoke billowed up from it like smoke from a furnace, the whole mountain trembled violently, and the sound of the trumpet grew louder and louder. Then Moses spoke and the voice of God answered him.

Exodus 20:18-21: When the people saw the thunder and lightning and heard the trumpet and saw the mountain in smoke, they trembled with fear. They stayed at a distance and said to Moses, "Speak to us yourself and we will listen. But do not have God speak to us or we will die." Moses said to the people, "Do not be afraid. God has come to test you, so that the fear of God will be with you to keep you from sinning." The people remained at a distance, while Moses approached the thick darkness where God was.

Exodus 24:17-18: To the Israelites the glory of the LORD looked like a consuming fire on top of the mountain. Then Moses entered the cloud as he

> **went on up the mountain. And he stayed on the mountain forty days and forty nights.**

In fact Moses became so intimate with I AM that, we are told, whenever Moses entered the tent of the meeting, the pillar of cloud would come down and stay, and "the LORD would speak to Moses face to face, as a man speaks with his friend" (Exodus 33:11). Moses became so close to the Lord and so desired his friendship, gracious kindness, and glory that he asked him, "Teach me your ways so I may know you and continue to find favor with you" (Exodus 33: 13), and, "Now show me your glory" (Exodus 33:18).

Contrast this with the rest of the Israelites who continued their worship from a distance, not because they were not allowed to go the tent of the meeting but because they chose not to go for whatever reason. Only Joshua came to the tent of meeting with Moses. Isn't it instructive that Joshua was the one chosen by the Lord to eventually lead the Israelites into the Promised Land?

Today's Exercise
Do you ever feel like the Israelites, wanting to worship the Lord at a distance, not wanting to come close to his light? Why or why not?

Prayer
Moses asked the Lord, "Teach me your ways so I may know you." Write a similar prayer in your own words. If this exercise evokes any kind of fear, be honest with the Lord and take courage from the example of Moses. Ask the Lord if there is anything he wants you to do in response.

Day 3
The Adulterous Woman

As we have discussed, and, as John affirms, Jesus is the pre-existent, incarnate light of the world throughout biblical history, Old and New Testament. Jesus' timing of each allegorical I AM is always instructive, and Jesus' proclamation that he is the light of the world is no exception. During the Feast of Tabernacles Jews from all over Israel, who had traveled to the temple, camped on the hills surrounding Jerusalem during the Feast. The Feast of the Tabernacles was a call for the Messiah and was a Festival marked by great joy, celebration, and light. The normally darkened hills that surrounded the temple were filled during the Festival with the beautiful light of camp fires and lanterns. How empty and void the hills of Jerusalem and the temple must have seemed at the conclusion of this joyous Festival. Just as Jesus is often most bright in our own lives during times of loss and emptiness it is here that Jesus first declared himself to be the light of the world.

In the very early morning after the Festival, Jesus, coming from the Mount of Olives, went back to the temple, and ALL the people came to hear him. What charisma and presence! Of course, he was, is God. I think it quite striking and singular how zealous the people were to hear and discuss the word of God. I wonder how many were in the temple at dawn.

Then the Pharisees brought an adulterous woman to him; another remarkable story of Jesus interacting with the women of his time—hated, despised, and sinful women.

> **John 8:1-2: But Jesus went to the Mount of Olives. At dawn he appeared again in the temple courts, where all the people gathered around him, and he sat down to teach them.**

Probably, the adulteress was caught in the act, in the dark, pre-dawn, when sin thrived on the exciting adrenalin and flickering candlelight of night. There was no way open for her to plead, "Not guilty." The Pharisees, as ever, tried to put Jesus in both a spiritual and secular quandary; by which, whatever they surmised, he could answer, he would condemn himself spiritually before the people and actually before the Roman occupiers of Israel. They posed the problem and the prescribed Mosaic sentence.

> John 8:3-6: The teachers of the law and the Pharisees brought in a woman caught in adultery. They made her stand before the group and said to Jesus, "Teacher, this woman was caught in the act of adultery. In the Law Moses commanded us to stone such women. Now what do you say?" They were using this question as a trap, in order to have a basis for accusing him.

The men, bringing the adulterous woman, were the intellects and scriptural scholars of their day, Pharisees, scribes, and elders. They wanted to get rid of Jesus, and as always, whether the issue was taxes, healing, or sin, they tried to put him in a position by which he would convict himself in such a way that his words would be a capital offense even to the Romans. They thought they had Jesus cornered, dead to rights. They believed they had outsmarted him. He had only two choices. He could adjudge the woman "guilty" or "not guilty."

"Thems the pickins', and there ain't no other!," as they say in Western literature and Oaters.

Jesus was known for dining with sinners, prostitutes, and even tax collectors like Matthew, the apostle. He had shared the greatest intimacy with them, his friendship and love. If he declared the woman to be guilty he became several things—a hypocrite, a liar, a usurper of Roman judicial authority (a capital offense.) He claimed to be a

week five

Messiah who came to save sinners and to offer reconciliation to all mankind. If he made a harsh judgment, he showed himself to be inconsistent with his proclamations and character, the character of a man who always gave mercy, forgiveness, and love.

On the other hand, if he chose a "not guilty" verdict, he appeared to conspire with sinners and wickedness, and, at last, with Satan himself. That would put him squarely against Mosaic law and all the prophets. His unholiness would be finally exposed, and he would be shown to be seeking the destruction of all the Jews held sacred. And he was still making judicial judgments reserved for the Romans. You know the Pharisees were saying to themselves, "We've got him. We've finally got him."

Now the Jews had the light of truth with them, and Jesus was in the darkness, maybe even the outer darkness. Jesus, with his great sense of story and himself, though, was going to bring the light of God's wisdom to this time and place and to forever. He didn't speak quickly. He stooped to write in the sand. Oh, how we wish we knew what he wrote. Many have surmised. But he showed the way, when being faced with a grave question, that we must all be slow, considered and thoughtful before speaking.

> **John 8:6: But Jesus bent down and started to write on the ground with his finger.**

Now he was ready to speak and shine the

In the law, there is a concept called "Clean Hands." It means that when you come to court you cannot be guilty of wrongdoing in the case you are bringing.

light of God's truth on all the accusers and on all of us. We are all sinners. God is so smart!

> John 8:7-8: When they kept on questioning him, he straightened up and said to them, "If any one of you is without sin, let him be the first to throw a stone at her." Again he stooped down and wrote on the ground.

None of us is without sin. We all sin and fall short of the grace of God as Paul tells us. In the law, there is a concept called "Clean Hands." It means that when you come to court you cannot be guilty of wrongdoing in the case you are bringing. You must come in with clean hands. If you don't have clean hands you can't bring the case. Jesus was the first to enunciate this doctrine. All the hearts of the accusers were convicted, first the elders. Perhaps as we grow older, we have had more time to sin, or perhaps we have gained the wisdom of knowing the truth when we hear it. In any event the older people began to leave first.

> John 8:9: At this, those who heard began to go away one at a time, the older ones first, until only Jesus was left, with the woman still standing there.

The woman knew she had been spared and had received grace, not judgment. She ad-

week five

dressed Jesus with deep respect. I like to think she even knew she had been forgiven by God. Jesus didn't let her off the hook about her future life, a sure sign of God's nature. He is not just about forgiveness but also repentance and turning away from our sin. He told her to leave and sin no more. He was strict but kind. Who could ask for a better parent or Messiah?

> John 8:10-11: Jesus straightened up and asked her, "Woman, where are they? Has no one condemned you?" "No one, sir," she said. "Then neither do I condemn you," Jesus declared. "Go now and leave your life of sin."

The timing, about Jesus' statement of himself as the light directly following this incident, is often questioned. Some scholars think it was later, perhaps even several days later. But I think it was directly following. After the woman left, the people returned to hear him speak, to perhaps listen to him explain his words. I think he used the occasion to again affirm himself as Messiah and as the light of wisdom. It seems to me appropriate that he do this when he had just illustrated so many character traits of the Messiah in his saving of the adulterous woman.

> John 8:12: When Jesus spoke again to the people, he said, "I AM the light of the world.

JESUS, THE LIGHT OF THE WORLD

> Whoever follows me will never walk in darkness, but will have the light of life."

Today's Exercise
What was the most meaningful part of today's lesson to you and why?

Prayer
Where do you need our Lord's light? Pray and ask him to bring his light to you.

173

Day 4
THE MAN BORN BLIND

J ohn, chapter nine, is devoted to one healing, the healing of a man born blind, experiencing the actual darkness in a world of light. Jesus healed the man, making clay from dirt, and then told him to wash in the pool of Siloam. Jon Courson makes this insightful point about Jesus' choice of mud to heal the man's eyes:

> *When Jesus put mud in the blind man's eyes, the man could have said, "Wait a minute. You're putting mud in my eye. You're not making things better—you're making them worse." Gang, many, many times the way of the Lord is to make things seem worse than they were before in order to get you to the place you really want to be: healed and seeing clearly. When the Lord muddies the waters, we usually don't know what He's doing. "I've been praying; I've been believ-*

ing, but things are only getting darker and dimmer.". . . But you know what mud does in one's eye? . . . it causes pain. So when Jesus said, "Go to the pool and wash," this guy didn't have to be asked twice. I don't believe his obedience was so much a statement of his great faith as it was a simple desire to get the mud out of his eye! . . . Maybe this week Jesus has allowed an irritation to come into your life that is causing you pain. . . . Here's what to do: Run quickly to the pool of Siloam, and you will receive your sight more clearly. . . . Where is the pool of Siloam? Jesus said, "You are clean through the Word which I have spoken unto you" (see John 15:3) Ephesians 5 says we are washed by the water of the Word."[2]

The man was obedient and received his healing on the Sabbath when Jews were forbidden to work. Neighbors and Pharisees asked the man how he received his sight.

> **John 9:13-17:** They (the neighbors of the man) brought to the Pharisees the man who had been blind. Now the day on which Jesus had made the mud

and opened the man's eyes was a Sabbath. Therefore the Pharisees also asked him how he had received his sight. "He put mud on my eyes," the man replied, "and I washed, and now I see." Some of the Pharisees said, "This man is not from God, for he does not keep the Sabbath." But others asked, "How can a sinner do such miraculous signs?" So they were divided. Finally they turned again to the blind man, "What have you to say about him? It was your eyes he opened." The man replied, "He is a prophet."

Jesus demonstrated, enlightened us that the Sabbath was made for man, for our rest and restoration, and was never meant to preclude the works of grace, mercy, and love of God. God is Grace, Mercy, and Love. We are always to do the works of God every day of the week. But doing his works on the Sabbath seems not only appropriate but our very special assignment and commandment. Jesus again put the Pharisees in an extremely untenable position. Healing the blind was a supernatural, miraculous work which the Old Testament pointed to as being a particular work of the Lord (Psalm 146:7-8, Isaiah 42:6-8). Yet the Pharisees claimed that only sinners worked on the

Sabbath. The Pharisees did everything they could to put out the light of Jesus. They professed not to believe the man, and then they called on his parents to support them. The parents were afraid of doing so for fear of being put out of the synagogue permanently (John 9:18-23).

I can relate here to the parents and their fear of people and authority. They did not want to offend the Pharisees for fear of their lives. If anyone proclaimed Jesus as Messiah, they were castigated and excommunicated. "Hey, talk to my son. He's the one who got healed. Don't look at me," would have been my response, too. Oh the courage of our Lord! He not only defied authority, he confronted it, challenged it, and always prevailed, even in death.

The Pharisees again summoned the man and put him in the position of blaspheming God if he wouldn't call Jesus a sinner. "Give Glory to God. Say this man (Jesus) is a sinner." You sense the anointing and reasoning of God in this man's words.

> John 9:24-25: A second time they summoned the man who had been blind. "Give glory to God," they said. "We know this man is a sinner." He replied, "Whether he is a sinner or not, I don't know. One thing I do know. I was blind but now I see!"

> "Whether he is a sinner or not, I don't know. One thing I do know. I was blind but now I see!"

The man put the Pharisees in the position of seeing by the light of God, a work of God, but calling it a work of Satan. So they retreated again to asking him what happened. The healed man was fed up and took the offensive. He asked them sarcastically if they wanted to become his disciples. Then when the Pharisees said they didn't even know where Jesus came from the man established Jesus firmly as a man of God who did the works of God.

John 9:26-33: Then they asked him, "What did he do to you? How did he open your eyes?" He answered, "I have told you already and you did not listen. Why do you want to hear it again? Do you want to become his disciples, too?" Then they hurled insults at him and said, "You are this fellow's disciple! We are disciples of Moses! We know that God spoke to Moses, but as for this fellow, we don't even know where he comes from." The man answered, "Now that is remarkable! You don't know where he comes from, yet he opened my eyes. We know that God does not listen to sinners. He listens to the godly man who does his will. Nobody has ever heard of opening the eyes of a

> man born blind. If this man were not from God, he could do nothing."

The Pharisees clearly needed to go back to debate school. They were losing every argument and finally always seemed to walk away, get very petulant, childish, wanting to excommunicate everyone who was a disciple of Jesus. But Jesus came to the rescue again and revealed to the man, his healer.

> **John 9:34-41:** To this they replied, "You were steeped in sin at birth; how dare you lecture us!" And they threw him out. Jesus heard that they had thrown him out, and when he found him, he said, "Do you believe in the Son of Man?" "Who is he, sir?" the man asked. "Tell me so that I may believe in him." Jesus said, "You have now seen him; in fact, he is the one speaking with you." Then the man said, "Lord, I believe," and he worshiped him. Jesus said, "For judgment I have come into this world, so that the blind will see and those who see will become blind." Some Pharisees who were with him heard him say this and asked,

> "What? Are we blind too?" Jesus said, "If you were blind, you would not be guilty of sin; but now that you claim you can see, your guilt remains."

Jesus was such a magnet for all that even some of the Pharisees were following him around. Jesus declaimed a last principle to them which made the undergarment and undergirding of those in authority very uncomfortable, downright scratchy. If we don't have the humility to acknowledge our ignorance, to be led into truth, our pride and stubbornness make our sin worse, and we can miss God all together. In short, pride makes us spiritually blind. Ouch! God's word has much to say on the issue of pride.

> Proverbs 11:2: When pride comes, then comes disgrace, but with humility comes wisdom.

> Proverbs 16:18-19: Pride goes before destruction, a haughty spirit before a fall. Better to be lowly in spirit and among the oppressed than to share plunder with the proud.

> Isaiah 66:2: This is the one I esteem: he who is humble and contrite in spirit, and trembles at my word.

week five

Ephesians 4:2: Be completely humble and gentle; be patient, bearing with one another in love.

James 4:10: Humble yourselves before the Lord, and he will lift you up.

Today's Exercise
What was the most meaningful part of today's lesson to you and why?

Prayer
Write a prayer about what was most meaningful to you today and ask the Lord if he wants you to do anything in response.

Day 5
CHILDREN OF THE LIGHT

> John 12:36, NLT: "Believe in the light while there is still time; then you will become children of the light." After saying these things, Jesus went away and was hidden from them.

There are a handful of people in my (Kim's) life who give me a special sense of belonging, of being included. Isn't it wonderful to feel that you belong? Jesus longs for his followers to feel a part of him and what he is doing; to know that we belong to his family; that we are his children; that he is the light, and we are the children of light. This week Jesus tells us that by believing in the light we will not only step out of darkness but we will become children of the light. The events leading up to Jesus' proclamation that we can become children of the light have much to teach us about being a child of the light.

> **John 12:20-22:** Now there were some Greeks among those who went up to worship at the Feast. They came to Philip, who was from Bethsaida in Galilee, with a request. "Sir," they said, "we would like to see Jesus." Philip went to tell Andrew; Andrew and Philip in turn told Jesus.

Around the time of the Feast when some Greeks came to Philip asking to "see" Jesus. They could see Jesus just as all the other people had been seeing Jesus, but obviously they wanted something special from him. Philip must have felt special himself at this point. He knew Jesus was becoming very popular, having raised Lazarus from the dead and having been hailed as a King with the waving of palms and the cries by the crowd of "Hosanna" (see John 12:12-15 NKJV).

Jesus really had become a celebrity. He was the King, the Messiah, the chosen one, about as high up on the Jerusalem "A list," as one can go, and those closest to him were basking in a little of his glory and his light. So Philip told Andrew about the Greeks and together they told Jesus, who replied to them:

> **John 12:23-26:** Jesus replied, "The hour has come for the Son of Man to be glorified. I tell you the truth, unless a ker-

> nel of wheat falls to the ground and dies, it remains only a single seed. But if it dies, it produces many seeds. The man who loves his life will lose it, while the man who hates his life in this world will keep it for eternal life. Whoever serves me must follow me; and where I am, my servant also will be. My Father will honor the one who serves me."

Here, Jesus talked about the opposite of life, light, and the joy of inauguration into his earthly kingship. He taught about death and giving up our self love of life and following him to eternal life. That must have been a real downer to Phillip and Andrew. They must have been scratching their heads at his response and wondering, "Jesus, did you even hear our question? The Greeks want to know if they can see you. They want to hear something extraordinary. I don't think they want to hear about seeds dying and losing one's life and serving. That doesn't sound a bit appealing or like anything anyone would want to do to become a child of light."

Of course, Jesus more than understood the question, and his reply literally handed the keys to his kingdom to his listeners if they could have understood. But they were in the dark and did not understand that it was not a physical kingdom they could see with their eyes, but a heavenly kingdom that they could only discern spiritually. When I read this scriptural passage over again, I realized that I would have been at least a bit frightened, thinking that he must be having a bad moment and would snap out of it. But his time was at hand, and he unveiled the true state of his heart. His listeners must have been, at the very least, surprised and disappointed and perhaps even some were dumbfounded especially considering his recent coronation. Then the darkness must have seemed to curl around the listeners like a fog when he said:

> John 12: 27-28: "Now my heart is troubled, and what shall I say? 'Father, save me from this hour?' No, it was for this very reason I came to this hour. Father, glorify your name!"

The hour of his greatest suffering was fast approaching wherein he would be the sin sacrifice for the sins of the whole world. But no one understood the meaning of his words. They did not understand the light and what he must do, at all. Christ said this, in full acceptance of his destiny, even though he was about to endure unspeakable humiliation, rejection, and physical agony, and even greater spiritual suffering when he would persevere through the full separation from his Father in order for the sins of the whole world and the wrath of his Father to go upon his whipped

week five

and frail physical body.

By this time, the time of the crucifixion, all the disciples had scattered, and Jesus' mother, her sister, Mary the wife of Cleophas, Mary Magdalene, and John were at the cross. Everyone had caved in to the darkness—disciples, high priests, elders, Pilate, the people, the Jews who had asked for the life of the criminal, Barabbas, in Jesus' place. The darkness fell, descended entirely upon all there at the cross. The fate of humanity hung in the balance, and it was solely on his shoulders. Our Lord cried out in some of the most poignant, sorrowful and anguished words of the Bible from Psalm 22:1:

> **My God, My God, why have You forsaken Me? (NKJV)**

Yet even in his physical agony he turned, as he always did, to the Father to regain his strength.

> **Luke 23:44-45: It was now about the sixth hour, and darkness came over the whole land until the ninth hour, for the sun stopped shining. And the curtain of the temple was torn in two. Jesus called out with a loud voice, "Father, into your hands I commit my spirit." When he had said this, he breathed his last.**

His mother, her sister, Mary the wife of Cleophas, Mary Magdalene, and John had witnessed the death of their precious Lord. Total darkness had fallen, the end of all things, of themselves even; they must have been thinking that the light had died. To them, it had been obliterated. Their creator had been killed. Jesus had told Philip, Andrew, the Greeks and the crowd about the light and the dark to come. They, very simply, did not understand. They were in the dark.

There, on the hill at Golgotha, the place of the skull, no one imagined, not a single person, that Jesus had just dealt the fatal blow to Satan, and that finally and forever he had broken the power of sin and death for all people, past, present, and future and ushered in the time of light forever. No one knew that what they thought was the darkest moment in their lives and perhaps the lives of all, the death of Jesus on the cross, was the moment of the coronation of the light, the life, the messiah, the king, and the brightest moment in all spiritual history. In, of course, the greatest irony of all time the crown of the savior of the world was a wreath of thorns and a mocking inscription on his cross, King of the Jews.

The people, all the crowds, the Greeks, the disciples, I think, as well, had hoped that the man they hailed as king would be with them physically forever, overthrow their Roman oppressors and take his place on the earthly throne of Israel. All seemed to be lost at the crucifixion. Dreams, hopes, promises must have seemed dashed in a million pieces. How could his followers now ever become children of light?

Well, dear ones, stand at the tomb with Mary Magdalene. She was not supposed to be there, and she must have been very scared and downhearted but courageously wanted to be close to him even in death. There was no light in her heart, but she went to the tomb in early morning while it was still dark.

> John 20:1-16: Early on the first day of the week, while it was still dark, Mary Magdalene went to the tomb and saw that the stone had been removed from the entrance. So she came running to Simon Peter and the other disciple, the one Jesus loved, and said, "They have taken the Lord out of the tomb, and we don't know where they have put him!" So Peter and the other disciple started for the tomb. Both were running, but the other disciple outran Peter and reached the tomb first. He bent over and looked in at the strips of linen lying there but did not go in. Then Simon Peter, who was behind him, arrived and went into the tomb. He saw the strips of linen lying there, as well as the

week five

Jesus longs for his followers to feel a part of him and what he is doing; to know that we belong to his family; that we are his children; that he is the light, and we are the children of light.

burial cloth that had been around Jesus' head. The cloth was folded up by itself, separate from the linen. Finally the other disciple, who had reached the tomb first, also went inside. He saw and believed. (They still did not understand from Scripture that Jesus had to rise from the dead.) Then the disciples went back to their homes, but Mary stood outside the tomb crying. As she wept, she bent over to look into the tomb and saw two angels in white, seated where Jesus' body had been, one at the head and the other at the foot. They asked her, "Woman, why are you crying?" "They have taken my Lord away," she said, "and I don't know where they have put him." At this, she turned around and saw Jesus standing there, but she did not realize that it was Jesus. "Woman," he said, "why are you crying? Who is it you are looking for?" Thinking he was the gardener, she said, "Sir, if you have carried him away, tell me where you have put him, and I will get him." Jesus said to her,

> "Mary." She turned toward him and cried out in Aramaic, "Rabboni!" (which means Teacher).

I am always so touched at how the Lord trusts and honors his women followers. Mary Magdalene (not Peter or John or the other apostles) was the first one to see the Lord after his death and the first one to receive the light of understanding, that Jesus Christ was resurrected to the glory of God the Father and the saving of humanity. The light dawned on her alone and then on the rest of the world. Good morning, Lord Jesus! I love the moment when she got the message, when the light of all the teachings of Jesus dawned on her. I have often gone to the cemetery to be near the ones I love. Have you done this? Isn't it interesting that we cling to the earthly remains of our loved ones? Mary wept with grief and love lost. The disciples left, although Jesus could have returned while they were still there. But he came to Mary alone. The coming of the light for the whole world, so intimate, so filled with compassion, tenderness, and love came through Mary to the whole world.

The light dawned. She understood that all he had been teaching was true with her calling out the simple appellation, "Rabboni." Mary was given the gift of seeing our Lord. But must we see to believe? Seeing is believing, or is it?

> **John 20:29:** Then Jesus told him, "Because you have seen

me, you have believed; blessed are those who have not seen and yet have believed."

2 Corinthians 4:18: So we fix our eyes not on what is seen, but on what is unseen. For what is seen is temporary, but what is unseen is eternal.

1 Peter 1:8-9: Though you have not seen him, you love him; and even though you do not see him now, you believe in him and are filled with an inexpressible and glorious joy, for you are receiving the goal of your faith, the salvation of your souls.

week five

Today's Exercise
Look over the last three verses. Which is the most meaningful verse to you and why?

Prayer
As Christ's followers we are called to walk by faith and not by sight. Write a prayer about areas in your life where you are having to walk by faith and not by sight. Like Jesus ask that the Father be glorified in your faith walk. Ask the Father to strengthen your

spirit and to give you spiritual eyes to see and to trust in Christ so you may be a light to all those around you.

Further Revelation
Write down any answers you had to prayer this week. What new revelations did you receive about our Lord? Write down any thoughts you have about this week.

week five

Weekly Exercise
Watch a sunset in a garden, a park, on a hill. Think about the dying of the light and what it meant and what it means in your life now. Think about darkness and light in your life right now. Invite the Lord to show you the light of his wisdom that will impact your life now. If you have the time watch the first stars come out. Enjoy the Lord's presence in both the light and dark.

WEEK SIX

Jesus, the Door to Life

*"The thief comes only to steal and kill and destroy;
I have come that they may have life,
and have it to the full." John 10:10*

week six

Day 1
OLD TESTAMENT DOORS

John 10:7-10: Therefore Jesus said again, "I tell you the truth, I AM the gate (door – NKJV) for the sheep. All who ever came before me were thieves and robbers, but the sheep did not listen to them. I AM the gate (door – NKJV); whoever enters through me will be saved. He will come in and go out, and find pasture. The thief comes only to steal and kill and destroy; I have come that they may have life, and have it to the full."

Jesus, the Door to Life

I knew I could not stay sober by myself. It is the one conclusion I had come to at the last of my drinking. But I was determined I would never go to a program for help which had a concept of God. I was an avowed atheist, even "devout," about the non-existence of God. As I later wrote in one of my novels, a fantasy satire, if God existed, he was a gross underachiever, a sadist, or a psychotic, the only determinations one could arrive at in this broken world.

I tried desperately to find a program which did not have a concept of God as a basis for recovery. I called *Women for Sobriety*, an organization for alcoholic women which depended solely on self-reliance and the group meetings for sobriety. I couldn't find them. I tried psychiatry. I enjoyed that, but it didn't keep me sober for even a day. I tried a rehab center which was not connected to AA or any God concepts, but they had just been taken over by a group espousing AA principles a week or two before I called. Finally, I seemed to have no choice. I felt I would have been on an endless search to find a door that either didn't exist or wouldn't open for me. I was bleak about all possibilities, but I knew I had to do something if I wanted to stay alive. So I called a friend of my mother's who was in AA, and she gave me the address of a church where AA meetings were held. Ironically, it is the church with the chapel where Jesus and I met, and the church for which I later became an acolyte.

I can remember standing at the door of the

church, right before the meeting, with a lot of shame and fear, at the gate to a different way of life. My wrists were bandaged from a suicide attempt. I tried to hide them with a long-sleeved shirt. My hair was in an Afro and stood out about six to eight inches on each side. How did I appear? I looked like an escapee from a lunatic asylum. I think I hoped I would be turned away and sent back for electric shock therapy. I stared at the door. *Wait a minute, I thought, I'll just attend this meeting, and then I don't have to come back.* For whatever reasons we come to the door, Jesus always says, "Welcome!" I went through the door, and I can now say with the psalmist:

> **Psalm 118:19-21: Open for me the gates of righteousness; I will enter and give thanks to the LORD. This is the gate of the LORD through which the righteous may enter. I will give you thanks, for you answered me; you have become my salvation.**

Gates and Doors in the Old Testament

The Old Testament is replete with the significance of gates and doors, both in particular and in general, in actuality and metaphorically. God warns Cain, a warning to us too, about sin crouching at our doors to our inner selves:

> **Genesis 4:6-7: Then the LORD said to Cain, "Why are you angry? Why is your face downcast? If you do what is right, will you not be accepted? But if you do not do what is right, sin is crouching at your door; it desires to have you, but you must master it."**

God told Noah to put a door in the Ark, by which life could pass through to safety. Jesus is our Ark.

> **Genesis 6:16: Put a door in the side of the ark and make lower, middle and upper decks.**

Lot opened his door and chose to house the angels of doom for Sodom and Gomorrah.

For slaves who wanted to stay with kind masters, Moses told them:

> **Deuteronomy 15:16-17: But if your servant says to you, "I do not want to leave you," because he loves you and your family and is well off with you,**

week six

then take an awl and push it through his ear lobe into the door, and he will become your servant for life. Do the same for your maidservant.

Here piercing your ear through to the door was the means of showing love for your master and devotion to your job. Symbolically, the psalmist used the lips as the door to speaking good or evil.

> **Psalm 141:3: Set a guard over my mouth, O LORD; keep watch over the door of my lips.**

In the Song of Solomon, the King, emblematic of our King, showed his love for the Shulamite woman by talking about treasures for her stored behind a door:

> **Song of Solomon 7:13: The mandrakes send out their fragrance, and at our door is every delicacy, both new and old, that I have stored up for you, my lover.**

The prophet Hosea was ordered by God to marry a harlot so that he would know how God felt about the harlotry of his people. But

Gates and doors open up new avenues of hope and spiritual adventure and love; they also shut down and shut out sin, betrayal, and death.

the Lord always holds out and is ready to open the door of hope.

> **Hosea 2:15: There I will give her (Israel) back her vineyards, and will make the Valley of Achor a door of hope.**

Much of God's business of mercy and justice was transacted at city gates. We see this, for instance, in Joshua where sanctuary was provided to the criminal who killed by accident.

> **Joshua 20:4: "When he (the murderer) flees to one of these cities, he is to stand in the entrance of the city gate and state his case before the elders of that city. Then they are to admit him into their city and give him a place to live with them."**

Ruth's marriage to Boaz brought children in the direct genealogy of David whose line was to sire and lead to the Messiah's eternal rule. Boaz transacted his right to marry Ruth at the town gate:

> **Ruth 4:1: Meanwhile Boaz went up to the town gate and sat there. When the kinsman-**

redeemer he had mentioned came along, Boaz said, "Come over here, my friend, and sit down." So he went over and sat down.

The book of Proverbs has much to say about the city gate, and its importance to the people. Proverbs 31 expresses the importance of the city gates to a godly woman and wife:

> Proverbs 31:23: Her (a godly woman's) husband is respected at the city gate, where he takes his seat among the elders of the land.

> Proverbs 31:31: Give her the reward she has earned, and let her works bring her praise at the city gate.

So gates and doors in the Old Testament open up new avenues of hope and spiritual adventure and love; they also shut down and shut out sin, betrayal and death; gates are the places people gather to dispense God's justice and mercy, to talk with each other about daily affairs, and to criticize but also praise and respect godly, deserving people.

JESUS, THE DOOR TO LIFE

Today's Exercise
Reflect back on your own life. How has Jesus used doors in your life? Consider the door of salvation, hope, protection, opportunity, love, adventure, fellowship, belonging, mercy, honor. . . . Write your thoughts about one or two doors Jesus has used in your life.

Prayer
What doors would you like opened today? Pray and ask Jesus to open this door for you.

week six

Day 2
More on the Passover

The most dramatic, prophetic and providential biblical utilization of doors in the Old Testament is found in Exodus 12:

Exodus 12:21-23: Then Moses summoned all the elders of Israel and said to them, "Go at once and select the animals for your families and slaughter the Passover lamb. Take a bunch of hyssop, dip it into the blood in the basin and put some of the blood on the top and on both sides of the doorframe. Not one of you shall go out the door of his house until morning. When the LORD goes through the land to strike down the Egyp-

> tians, he will see the blood on the top and sides of the doorframe and will pass over that doorway, and he will not permit the destroyer to enter your houses and strike you down."

The final and tenth plague upon the Egyptians was the killing of all their firstborn. The means of distinguishing the Israelites from the Egyptians, and the saving of the Israelites from the death of their firstborn, foretells the death of Jesus in every respect. He is our Passover Lamb and his blood on the doorway to our spiritual selves saves us. On a daily basis I say, as part of my morning prayer, "I wash in the blood of Jesus." I am symbolically sprinkling, more like dousing my doorframe in the blood of the Lamb, Jesus, for protection against the destroyer. Where the blood of the lamb has been applied, the place, our inner self, becomes completely protected. God holds his people sacred and separate, marked for salvation by the blood of Jesus. When God saw the blood on the doors of the Israelites he spared all the families within those houses. The use of the hyssop to apply the blood to the houses of the Israelites was part of the consecration, purification, and salvation of the Israelites. Keil and Delitzsch Commentary on the Old Testament says:

week six

> *But the smearing of the doorposts and lintel with blood, the house was expiated (made atonement for sin) and consecrated on an altar. That the smearing with blood was to be regarded as an act of expiation, is evident from the simple fact, that a hyssop-bush was used for the purpose (v. 22); for sprinkling with hyssop is never prescribed in the law, except in connection with purification in the sense of expiation (Leviticus 14:49 ff.; Numbers 19:18-19).*[1]

So God's covenant with the Israelites was that if he saw the blood upon their doors, they would be saved; they would be delivered. In the New Covenant we are rescued by our belief in God's promise that the sacrifice and shed blood of his only begotten Son would deliver us (John 3:16).

> John 3:16: For God so loved the world that he gave his one and only Son, that whoever believes in him shall not perish but have eternal life.

Jesus' death follows exactly the night of Passover for the Israelites including the hyssop branch.

When Jesus said the words, "It is finished," his work of redemption, restoration, salvation, and reconciliation was done and completed forever.

207

> John 19:28-30: Later, knowing that all was now completed, and so that the Scripture would be fulfilled, Jesus said, "I am thirsty." A jar of wine vinegar was there, so they soaked a sponge in it, put the sponge on a stalk of the hyssop plant, and lifted it to Jesus' lips. When he had received the drink, Jesus said, "It is finished." With that, he bowed his head and gave up his spirit.

The doors of Jesus' lips, our blood sacrifice, sprinkled with the hyssop attests that all the spiritual houses of mankind are consecrated and salvaged from ruin and destruction, if we choose. When Jesus said the words, "It is finished," his work of redemption, restoration, salvation, and reconciliation was done and completed forever. He could bow his head and give up his spirit because his earthly mission, his perfect sacrifice was complete.

week six

Today's Exercise
Do you ever feel guilty for past sins you have already confessed and turned away from? Well, you need to be finished with feeling guilty. Jesus proclaimed that the penalty for that sin was paid in full when he said, "It is finished." Don't reject his gift of forgiveness, but rather embrace it with all that you are. Journal on any thoughts you have below.

Prayer
Take this time to confess to the Lord any unconfessed sins you have committed. Commit to turning away from this sin. Then sit and bask in God's finished work and receive his total forgiveness and acceptance.

Ongoing/Lifestyle Sins
If you are stuck in a lifestyle of sin—whether it be an addiction, sexual immorality, unforgiveness, bitterness, anger, or hatred—bring this before the Lord and ask him for the door to turn away for this sinful lifestyle and to begin to break free from this sin. Confess this sin to a trusted friend, pastor, or church leader and ask them to help you find a recovery path that will help you break free from this area of sin. Leave the door open to all the Lord may want to bring into your life to

help you break free. This may be in the form of the Bible study like *Breaking Free* by Beth Moore, a recovery program like Celebrate Recovery, books, counseling, intensive counseling weekends by New Life, support groups, and/or some combination of the above. And remember:

Galatians 5:1: It is for freedom that Christ has set us free. Stand firm, then, and do not let yourselves be burdened again by a yoke of slavery.

Day 3
THE NARROW GATE

Jesus is our perfect offering and through his sacrifice we can enter the gate of eternal life. This gate will not be opened by all, for Jesus tells us in Matthew 7:13-14:

> "Enter through the narrow gate. For wide is the gate and broad is the road that leads to destruction, and many enter through it. But small is the gate and narrow the road that leads to life, and only a few find it."

To open the Jesus Gate we must believe in him and choose to travel with him down the road of righteousness, a rocky road by which we are summoned to move in the footsteps of our Lord down narrow and steep paths where slips and falls are many. For years I chose the wide gate and broad and spacious road, the

week six

fastest lane on the autobahn in an expensive Lamborghini sin car. I ran my sports car into a ditch, and Jesus pulled me out and sent me through the small gate to sin rehab. Thank God for God! No, life as a Christian is not a cakewalk, and every day I must choose to enter through the narrow gate. The passage preceding Matthew 7:13 tells me what it means to enter through the narrow gate:

> **Matthew 7:12: "So in everything, do to others what you would have them do to you, for this sums up the Law and the Prophets."**

When we enter the narrow gate we will not be following a direct path with road rules and regulations marked out and clearly stated. We will not be taking a vacation tour. AAA gives out marked maps, books, and plans for your trips with everything you need to do to have a successful trip. Our trip will not be clearly marked out by maps, books, and plans; rather we will be on the Jesus journey. We just get through the Jesus Gate and get on the Jesus road and there will be no road signs; only our travel guide Jesus to point the way each day. Oh, and one more thing we are supposed to be treating everyone, all fellow travelers, the way we wish to be treated. Pretty simple and easy!

I don't think so. I've done a lot of pushing,

Jesus, the Door to Life

> We just get through the Jesus Gate and get on the Jesus road and there will be no road signs; only our travel guide Jesus to point the way each day.

shoving, bribing, taking illegal detours, cutting off other cars to get in the turn lane, shouting and bullying along the way, but slowly and surely I seem to be learning and walking more like my travel guide.

Today, there appear to be many doors and many luscious boulevards to heaven, to God. Jesus makes it crystal clear that there is only one door to God the Father, one door to eternal life and he, Jesus, is that door. That being said, Jesus can use whatever he wants to draw people to himself, and we need to be careful that we don't shut doors that Jesus may be using to beckon others to himself. The founders of AA, Bill W and Dr. Bob, were both Christian but decided that for people to get sober they had to be able to believe in their own conception of God. Though AA is not a Christian organization it was the door that led me to Jesus. I found that in the end, if we disavow the Lord and insist on another way as did the Pharisees and many of the synagogue elders, then we become criminals, thieves, and robbers:

> **John 10:1: "I tell you the truth, the man who does not enter the sheep pen by the gate, but climbs in by some other way, is a thief and a robber."**

Jesus used doors in some of his parables to caution us to enter through the narrow gate.

week six

Matthew 25:1-13: "At that time the kingdom of heaven will be like ten virgins who took their lamps and went out to meet the bridegroom, five of them were foolish and five were wise. The foolish ones took their lamps but did not take any oil with them. The wise, however, took oil in jars along with their lamps. The bridegroom was a long time in coming, and they all became drowsy and fell asleep. At midnight the cry rang out: 'Here's the bridegroom! Come out to meet him!' Then all the virgins woke up and trimmed their lamps. The foolish ones said to the wise, 'Give us some of your oil; our lamps are going out.' 'No,' they replied, 'there may not be enough for both us and you. Instead, go to those who sell oil and buy some for yourselves.' But while they were on their way to buy the oil, the bridegroom arrived. The virgins who were ready went in with him to the wedding banquet. And the door was shut. Later the others also came. 'Sir!

> Sir!' they said. 'Open the door for us!' But he replied, 'I tell you the truth, I don't know you.' Therefore keep watch, because you do not know the day or the hour."

The door of salvation, the narrow gate, is a gift of grace that comes through faith in Jesus, our savior. We cannot enter the narrow gate by good works but only through our faith in Jesus. However, in the following passages, Jesus is telling us here that if we enter through the narrow gate and accept him as savior it will be evident in our lives. We will have a desire to know him, a desire to please him, a desire to follow him, and, though we are not perfect, we will naturally become more like him. We will want to obey his commands because we know him. Knowing Jesus is to love him, and to love him is to obey him. Obedience is a natural outflow of knowing Jesus.

> John 8:31-32: Jesus said, "If you hold to my teaching, you are really my disciples. Then you will know the truth, and the truth will set you free."

> John 14:21: "Whoever has my commands and obeys them, he is the one who loves me. He

who loves me will be loved by my Father, and I too will love him and show myself to him."

Today's Exercise
What part of today's lesson is most meaningful to you and why?

Prayer
Write a prayer in response to what was meaningful to you today and ask the Lord if there is anything he wants you to do in response.

Day 4
THE DOOR OF PROTECTION

Be careful of the door you choose to open! In the movie, *Leaving Las Vegas*, a man chooses to commit suicide by drinking himself to death. He sells all that he has and finally closes the door of the house where he lived in Los Angeles, leaving it for good, and goes to Las Vegas to drink himself to death, opening a lot of doors to shabby motel rooms where he can wallow in the disease of alcoholism.

Who makes that kind of stupid, self-annihilating choice? I did. Some days I could not even get out the door of my bedroom I was so sick with alcohol poisoning. I may not have said the words, but, I knew deep inside myself, I was dying by inches and sometimes whole yards with my alcoholic life. But, as I lay in my bed in my bedroom, with alcoholic migraine and nausea, I did say a prayer. I didn't know at the time it was a prayer, and I didn't know there was anyone there to hear. BUT THERE WAS, AND WE KNOW WHO IT WAS. I said, as I looked out my window, to a bare tree appearing to be like a black demon with fangs, "Oh, I wish there were a God because I would ask him to show me a way (a door) to quitting drinking and to living. Oh I wish there were a God!"

He showed me; he was the door of AA. How do I know this? I think about my life today. My life now is very abundant with lots of freedom and joy, friends, and family and pastures of repose often by the bumpy road of life. Jesus keeps his promises.

> John 10:7-10: Therefore Jesus said again, "I tell you the truth, I AM the gate (door – NKJV) for the sheep. All who ever came before me were thieves and robbers, but the sheep did not listen to them. I AM the gate (door – NKJV); whoever enters through me will be saved. He will come in and go out, and find pasture. The thief comes only to steal and kill and destroy; I have come that they may have life, and have it to the full."

JESUS, THE DOOR TO LIFE

Thieves versus Shepherds

John 10:1-5: "I tell you the truth, the man who does not enter the sheep pen by the gate, but climbs in by some other way, is a thief and a robber. The man who enters by the gate is the shepherd of his sheep. The watchman opens the gate for him, and the sheep listen to his voice. He calls his own sheep by name and leads them out. When he has brought out all his own, he goes on ahead of them, and his sheep follow him because they know his voice. But they will never follow a stranger; in fact, they will run away from him because they do not recognize a stranger's voice."

Jesus is the gate, and he is the good shepherd, the subject of the next chapter. In order to understand how Jesus could be both the shepherd and the gate, an overview of shepherding in the time of Jesus is very instructive. Often shepherds would put their sheep in a communal sheepfold at night. Then they would appoint a shepherd who became the watchman for the sheep over night. The watchman/shepherd would then lie down at night to block the entrance to the sheepfold so no one could come in or out including the sheep. The shepherd literally became the gate to the sheepfold. In the morning the other shepherds would return and be let in to the sheepfold by the watchman/shepherd. Each shepherd would call out his own sheep. The sheep knew the voice of their own shepherd and would follow their own shepherd when called. Thieves would never come in through the entrance, but would climb over the walls or bushes of the sheepfold and toss the sheep over the wall to their conspirators. This gives us a picture of Jesus as our shepherd and our gate but also of thieves and other church shepherds, pastors, and elders. We learn several characteristics about a true shepherd in these first passages of John 10.

First, the only means of entrance to the sheep pen is through Jesus Christ. The driving inspiration of each shepherd is for the welfare of his sheep. There is no other way; certainly no secular way with all its selfish, avaricious desires. So motivations of any other interest than to serve Jesus and his people is reprehensible and shameful, completely dishonorable in the kingdom of God and only obtained by forced, illegal entry.

The man who comes by the gate of Jesus Christ will be the shepherd of his sheep.

> The thief comes only to steal and kill and destroy I have come that they may have life, and have it to the full.

> John 10:2: "The man who enters by the gate is the shepherd of his sheep."

Second, this shepherd, according to this allegorical insight, has a calling by the watchman who is Jesus. Each shepherd has his own voice and the sheep, under this shepherd, respond to his call. So the pastor has an intimate relationship with his parish, and the parish knows the rightness of his theology and preaching in Jesus Christ.

> John 10:3: "The watchman opens the gate for him, and the sheep listen to his voice. He calls his own sheep by name and leads them out."

Third, the pastor, once through the gate, is the leader of his pastorate, fully in command of his theology of Jesus Christ and speaking it out in such a way that his congregation has no doubt of the firmness of his right thinking and hence theirs.

> John 10:4: "When he has brought out all his own, he goes on ahead of them, and his sheep follow him because they know his voice."

week six

I think we see today the tragic results of those who have followed a stranger's voice. There was Waco; and the cult who killed themselves with the appearance of the Comet Hale Bopp; terrorists who believe God is a god of hatred and revenge; sects who follow gurus claiming to be THE CHRIST like Jim Jones and conform to his precepts, even suicide. The list goes on and on. The pastor who understands and exalts Jesus as the atonement for the sins of humanity, his is the voice we know to speak the truth.

> **John 10:5: "But they (the sheep congregation) will never follow a stranger; in fact, they will run away from him because they do not recognize a stranger's voice."**

How do we guard against following a different shepherd's voice than our own shepherd? We distinguish between voices. We know the voice of our shepherd.

How do we come to know the voice of the shepherd? Some of the ways to knowing his voice are: going to a church where the biblical teaching is sound; studying the Bible; spending time with others who know the voice of the shepherd; praying and taking time to listen to the shepherd's voice within.

Today's Exercise
Often, when we are studying Scripture such as the I AM sayings, certain passages and teachings are particularly meaningful to us. They almost seem to jump off the page. The shepherd frequently speaks to us by this means of highlighting. Take some time to go over your answers to the Today's Exercise in the last several weeks. What has the shepherd been showing and saying to you?

Prayer
Begin by asking the shepherd to enable you to hear his voice clearly. Write a prayer in response to what has been meaningful to you recently as you have been studying I AM and ask the Lord if there is anything he wants you to do in response?

Day 5
THE DOOR OF INTIMACY

Revelation 3:20: "Here I AM! I stand at the door and knock. If anyone hears my voice and opens the door, I will come in and eat with him, and he with me."

Being safely behind the door of protection of God comes through knowing our Savior. Studying the Word of God is one of the primary ways and doors to come to know Jesus, which will not only lead to our protection but a growing closeness with him. Drawing near to our shepherd also comes through the door of prayer. It is no coincidence that Jesus spent a good amount of time teaching his followers how to pray, beckoning each one of them to open the door, and then actually to close the door in order to pray and to be intimate with God the Father behind the closed door.

week six

Praying in Secret

> Matthew 6:6: "But when you pray, go into your room, close the door and pray to your Father, who is unseen. Then your Father, who sees what is done in secret, will reward you."

Andrew Murray, in his classic work on prayer, *With Christ in the School of Prayer*, makes the following observations concerning this passage:

> *The first thing in the closet-prayer is to meet the Father. The light that shines in the closet must be the light of the Father's countenance. The atmosphere in which we breath and pray is God's Father-love, God's infinite Fatherliness. Thus, each thought or petition we breathe out will be in simple, hearty, and childlike trust in the Father.*

> *Thus we are taught at the very beginning of our search for the secret of effective prayer to remember that it is in the inner chamber, where we are alone with the Father, that we learn*

> It is no coincidence that Jesus spent a good amount of time teaching his followers how to pray, beckoning each one of them to open the door, . . .

> *to pray properly. The Father is in secret. In these words, Jesus teaches us where He is waiting for us and where He is always to be found.*[2]

More than any generation in history, we are a generation of constant interruption and demands. All of us feel we are on call 24-7 and that whoever needs us must have access to us at all times. This is beautifully illustrated by a dear friend of mine whose son began college very far from their home. On his first day of college he got lost and called his mom for help. Even though she was over a thousand miles away she felt obligated to immediately stop what she was doing and to go online to find a map of the campus so she could help him find his first class. I think, to one degree or another, we can all relate to her sense of obligation to be on call. It is almost unfathomable that humanity even got to the late 20th century without cell phones, but it is good to remind ourselves of this fact.

I believe this can easily result in our being more disconnected with ourselves and God than ever. It is vital for us to take time to shut out the entire world including our cell phones and meet with our Heavenly Father in private. This gives us room to just be his children and to cast all our worries on him in order to be equipped, strengthened, refreshed, and to, most of all, just enjoy his company.

week six

Open the Door

Revelation 3:20: "Here I AM! I stand at the door and knock. If anyone hears my voice and opens the door, I will come in and eat with him, and he with me."

Though this Scripture is often quoted in the context of Jesus' knocking at the door of a nonbeliever's heart, it is actually addressed to believers. Why is Jesus outside the house of a believer needing to knock to come in? John Courson says in his *Application Commentary New Testament*:

> *What happened here is something that can happen to us. . . . It's the danger of doctrinal drowsiness that says, "Lord, I know You're calling me to come away this morning and seek You. But I'm yours and You're mine . . . so I'll meet with you a little later . . . zzz . . ." [W]hen He called to us we chose to say, "I don't need to go to Bible study. I don't need devotions this morning. . . ."*

and then actually to close the door in order to be intimate with God the Father behind the closed door.

> *There's a tragic self-centeredness to which the bride is vulnerable—especially after she's been a bride for a while. It's not about how we're doing. It's about how willing we are to dirty our feet, open the door and give to others . . .*
>
> *[Then] I'll be wondering where the Lord is and why I'm not sensing His presence, when suddenly there's someone for me to tell about Him. And sure enough, as I talk about Him, I experience intimacy with Him.*
>
> *Dear sister, precious brothers—the key to intimacy to your Christian walk, the source of enough spiritual energy to skip on the mountains of fellowship and share with you neighbors . . . is to say "YES" when the Bridegroom knocks at your door.*[3]

You would think that because I write books about the Bible that spiritual complacency would be far from me. Not so. Amazingly, I can spend a whole day studying Scripture and writing about Christ without ever taking time to fellowship with him or to be involved with his people. Today's Scripture reading is a wonderful reminder to us about how we cheat ourselves when we fail to walk through the door of intimacy with Jesus.

Today's Exercise
What part of today's lesson is most meaningful to you and why?

Prayer
Write a prayer in response to what was meaningful to you today and ask the Lord if there is anything he wants you to do in response?

Further Revelation
Write down any answers you had to prayer this week. What new revelations did you receive about our Lord? Write down any thoughts you have about this week.

Weekly Exercise
Walk through the door of intimacy with our Lord by spending at least 30 minutes sitting quietly before Him. Spend your time asking for what you need but also seek to hear from our Lord. Ask him what he would like to show you, what he would like to reveal about himself for you to have a deeper understanding of his great love for you (Ephesians 3:18). Sometimes reading a devotional and a Bible passage is a wonderful way to enter that door of intimacy with our Lord.

Introduction

1. Hannah W. Smith, *The God of All Comfort* (Chicago, IL: Moody Press, 1956 Edition), 20.

Chapter 1 – I AM in the Book of Exodus

1. Hannah W. Smith, *The God of All Comfort* (Chicago, IL: Moody Press, 1956 Edition), 20.

2. Exodus 3:14, Adam Clarke's Commentary, Electronic Database. Copyright© 1996 by Biblesoft.

3. Ibid.

4. *Nelson's Illustrated Bible Dictionary*, Copyright© 1986, Thomas Nelson Publishers.

5. Edward Schillebeeckx, translated by John Bowden, *Christ, The Experience of Jesus as Lord* (New York, NY: Crossroad Publishing Company, 1986), 89.

6. Hannah W. Smith, *The God of All Comfort* (Chicago, IL: Moody Press, 1956 Edition), 20.

Chapter 2 – I AM in the Book of John. I AM Stands alone, Jesus as I AM

1. John 1:1, *The NIV Life Application Bible Commentary, Life Applicaton Study Bible*, New International Version, Copyright© 1997, Tyndale House Publishers Inc. and Zondervan Publishing House, p. 1734.

2. Ibid.

3. John 8:28, *Matthew Henry's Commentary on the Whole Bible*, PC Study Bible Formatted Electronic Database, Copyright© 2006 by Biblesoft, Inc. All Rights reserved.

4. John 8:28-29, *Matthew Henry's Commentary on the Whole Bible*, PC Study Bible Formatted Electronic Database Copyright© 2006 by Biblesoft, Inc. All Rights reserved.

⁵ John 8:56, *Adam Clarke's Commentary*, Electronic Database. Copyright© 1996 by Biblesoft.

⁶ Psalm 41:9 explaining John 13:18-19, Jon Courson, *Jon Courson's Application Commentary Old Testament, Volume 2* (Nashville, TN: Thomas Nelson Publishers, Copyright© 2005), 51; and Jon Courson, *Jon Courson's Application Commentary New Testament* (Nashville, TN: Thomas Nelson Publishers, Copyright© 2005), 549.

⁷ Psalm 22, Isaiah 52, 53, *Nelson's Illustrated Bible Dictionary*, Nashville, TN: Thomas Nelson Publishers, Copyright© 1986.

Chapter 3 – I AM in the Book of John. Jesus Tells Us Who He is and Who We Are in Him

¹ John 7:28-29, *Adam Clarke's Commentary*, Electronic Database. Copyright© 1996 by Biblesoft.

² Henry T. Blackaby and Claude V. King, *Experiencing God* (Nashville, TN: Lifeway Press, 1990), 19.

³ John 17:24, Jamieson, Fausset, and Brown Commentary, Electronic Database. Copyright© 1997 by Biblesoft.

⁴ John 17:24, Jamieson, Fausset, and Brown Commentary, Electronic Database. Copyright© 1997 by Biblesoft.

Chapter 4 – I AM THE BREAD OF LIFE in the Book of John

No footnotes for this chapter.

Chapter 5 – I AM THE LIGHT OF THE WORLD in the Book of John

¹ Genesis 1:3-5, *Matthew Henry's Commentary on the Whole Bible*, PC Study Bible Formatted Electronic Database Copyright© 2006 by Biblesoft, Inc. All Rights reserved.

² John Courson, *Jon Courson's Application Commentary New Testament* (Nashville, TN: Thomas Nelson Publishers, Copyright© 2005), 519-520.

Chapter 6 – I AM THE GATE FOR THE SHEEP in the Book of John

¹ Exodus 12:22, *Keil & Delitzsch Commentary on the Old Testament: New Updated Edition*, Electronic Database. Copyright© 1996 by Hendrickson Publishers, Inc.

² Matthew 6:6, Andrew Murray, *With Christ in the School of Prayer*, (New Kensington, PA: Whitaker House, Copyright© 1981), 24-25.

³ Revelation 3:20, John Courson, *Jon Courson's Application Commentary New Testament* (Nashville, TN: Thomas Nelson Publishers, Copyright© 2005), 1691.

237

About the Authors

Diana Burg

Mother, Diana Burg, and daughter, Kim Tapfer have had an amazing and miraculous journey together to the writing of this study on discipleship. They have debated whether or not to tell their story with all the messy, sad, and sometimes very tragic consequences and plights that resulted, as they always do, from dealing with an outrageous and out-of-control alcoholic in your family. But in May of 1979, when Kim was 13 years old, Diana went to her first Alcoholics Anonymous meeting.

Isn't it always fascinating, often paradoxical and enigmatic, how the Lord's redemption and restoration work? Diana was a hardened atheist who searched for help with her alcoholism in every possible place, every nook and cranny in the world, except Alcoholics Anonymous because AA required, in their third step, that your life be turned over to God. But, at that point, she was desperate for help with her drinking. So she went to AA.

Kim had met a neighbor friend, Cherie, several years earlier, who had told her all about Jesus, and she decided to give her life to the Lord Jesus around the time Diana went to AA. She asked her mother early on in AA, one day, to look into the possibility that Jesus was Lord and Savior and promised eternal life because she knew her mother was afraid of death.

Kim Tapfer

So Diana went to a small chapel sometime in 1979, where she met the Lord and felt the presence of the Holy Spirit and there gave her life to the Lord.

Kim is an attorney and lives with her husband, Ted, and their two children, Brad and Mandy, in Newport Beach, California. She has been involved in Bible Studies for many years as a leader, teacher and speaker, and she currently leads a women's Bible study at her church, Mariners, in Irvine, California.

Diana has lived all her life in Denver and resides in its foothills with her husband and father of Kim, Charles. For a number of years she was on staff with a ministry teaching Bible studies on hearing the voice of God. She also became an acolyte—someone who assists the priest during services with readings from the Bible and serving Communion—in the Episcopal Church. She has written several books—*Getting to Know God* and *Mourning Glory* published by BurgYoung, and an historical novel *Dalliance* published by Syracuse University Press.

Mother and daughter wanted to share their passion for the Lord and his Word by writing something together. Diana had written a book on the I AM sayings of Jesus. After much prayer and discussion they decided to write a meditative Bible study based on Diana's book, and so *I AM – a Meditative Bible Study on the I AM Sayings of Jesus* was born. The first volume of the work is a six-week Bible study as described in the introduction. They both believe it is a work for people seeking a deeper walk and wanting to experience greater transformation through an intimate relationship with Christ. We ask blessings and enlightenment, joy and depth—deep calling to deep—for all the students of this work.

Notes ~ week one

Notes ~ week two

Notes ~ week three

Notes ~ week four

Notes ~ week five

Notes ~ week six

www.ingramcontent.com/pod-product-compliance
Lightning Source LLC
LaVergne TN
LVHW051043080426
835508LV00019B/1681